D0458276

Hold On,
But Don't Hold Still

life

Hold On,
But Don't Hold Still

Hope and Humor
from My Seriously
Flawed Life

Kristina Kuzmič

VIKING LIFE

VIKING
An imprint of Penguin Random House LLC
penguinrandomhouse.com

A Viking Life Book

Grateful acknowledgment is made to the following for permission to reprint:
"If I Could" written by Marti Sharron, Ken Hirsch, and Ron Miller.
© 1988 Sony/ATV Music Publishing LLC, EMI Blackwood Music Inc., and
The Helene C. Hemminger Trust (ASCAP). All rights on behalf of Sony/ATV Music
Publishing LLC and EMI Blackwood Music Inc. administered by Sony/ATV Music
Publishing LLC. Rights on behalf of The Helene C. Hemminger Trust
administered by Wixen Music Publishing, Inc.
All rights reserved. Used by permission.

LIBRARY OF CONGRESS CATALOGING-IN-PUBLICATION DATA

Names: Kuzmič, Kristina, author.
Title: Hold on, but don't hold still: hope and humor from
my seriously flawed life / Kristina Kuzmič.
Description: First edition. | New York: Viking Life [2020]
Identifiers: LCCN 2019031040 | ISBN 9780525561842 (hardcover) |
ISBN 9780525561859 (ebook)
Subjects: LCSH: Kuzmič, Kristina. | Single mothers—United
States—Biography. | Motherhood—Humor. | Self-acceptance. |
Self-realization. | Success.
Classification: LCC HQ759.915 .K89 2020 | DDC 306.874′32 [B]—dc23
LC record available at https://lccn.loc.gov/2019031040

Printed in the United States of America
1   3   5   7   9   10   8   6   4   2

DESIGNED BY MEIGHAN CAVANAUGH

To the most meaningful chapters of my story,

my children: Luka, Matea, and Ari

Contents

Introduction

There's a name for when things don't work out the way you thought they would. It's called "life."

I'm known by my viewers as the "funny mom," the mom who finds humor in every nook and cranny of motherhood while shoving brownies in her mouth and drinking coffee straight out of a coffeepot. I love humor. I need humor. Tackling life without it is like trying to eat soup with a fork. Sure, you'll still get a tiny bit of nourishment from eating that way, but you'll miss out on so much goodness. Before I could laugh about being a mom or embrace the mind-bending challenges of life, I needed something much more vital and basic: I needed hope.

Thirteen years ago, I was a single mom sharing a bedroom with my two rambunctious, wonderful, exhausting young children. I was juggling two jobs and taking every shortcut I could, including not being too proud to accept breakfast help from my friend who worked at Starbucks and let me have the leftover, stale pastries that were no longer fit for their display case.

On one particularly stressful morning a few years into my parenting gig and not long after my divorce, I was awoken by the loud clang of two human alarm clocks—my two- and three-year-olds. Sleep deprivation, plus a lack of personal space and time, can often make one feel like they're having a hangover—a parenting hangover. I hadn't had anything to drink the night before, but I had consumed so much of my anxiety and tears that I felt completely disoriented come morning. I'd been up late, hunched over next to my kids' bunk beds, gathering documents and filling out paperwork for a big adventure I had scheduled for the following day.

That morning, after buckling the kids in their car seats, I pleaded with them to please make sure at least 80 percent of their muffins (the previously mentioned Starbucks treat) ended up in their mouths and not on their clothes or the floor of my car. And off we went on our adventure.

Life tip: always refer to stress-inducing appointments as adventures.

Our "adventure" that morning was at the Department of Social Services. A few days prior, I had sold my old wedding ring to cover that month's rent, and now I was hoping to be approved for food stamps. Other than my car—which I needed in order to get to my jobs—I was fresh out of valuable possessions I could sell in order to help pay the bills.

When my name was called, my lovely children were pin-balling around the waiting area as if they were hooked up to an IV of pure sugar. I scooped them up, one kid in each arm, and walked to the window to turn over my paperwork. The woman working there curtly fired a string of questions at me, glanced over the documents I'd painstakingly compiled, and didn't once even bother to lift her head to look me in the eye. Not being able to provide the basics for my children made me feel worthless. Not being treated like a human deserving of eye contact by the woman standing between me and the resources I needed only amplified my self-loathing. I wondered for a second what her life was like. Had she ever felt depressed and lonely and overwhelmed and broke and suicidal like I did? Did she have children she loved more than anything in the whole wide world? Did she feel they deserved so much better than what she could ever offer?

Hours later, flooded with relief but also reeling with shame, the kids and I were back in the little room we shared. I could barely hold in the surge of sadness that started to consume me as I wrestled Matea out of her shoes and coat while attempting to coax Luka to just try going potty before naptime. In the midst of this chaos, Matea gently grabbed my cheeks in her tiny hands. She looked deeply into my eyes with her big brown ones and said, "Mommy, I wuv your cute widdle face." My heart burst. How did she know I needed that love right then, at that moment?

"Baby girl, you are so sweet." My eyes filled with tears now. "I love you and I love when you grab my face like that with your precious little hands."

And with her hands still planted firmly on my cheeks, she said with her cute lisp, "I have boogers in my hands." (Before kids, that would have been gross. After kids? Just a normal Tuesday.)

Once the kids were finally down for their nap, I picked up one of the many books I had been reading. I wasn't a big reader growing up, much to the dismay of my scholarly parents. My father once risked his life in a plane crash because he refused to slide down the emergency exit without first grabbing his books. He was the last passenger to exit the plane, clinging to his bag of books. But I didn't inherit my father's addiction to reading. I had always been too antsy to sit still with a book. Or to sit still at all. Until one day, I wasn't.

I'm not sure if my eyes needed a break from crying or my mind craved distraction from the utter failure that had become my life, but I was suddenly captivated by reading. Hope was the common thread that kept me turning the pages of the books I found—books about other women whose lives looked nothing like mine but who were chasing down and finding the same solace I was after: hope.

I spent many nights on the floor next to my kids' beds, counting my waitressing tips to make sure I had enough to cover bills that month, feeling like a worthless mom, escaping into my books when the days became too much, so cried out and screamed out that I was becoming numb to it all. The bad, the really bad, the occasional good, the status quo. It all felt the same. It all felt like nothing.

And then one day I found the guts to stop floating through my life like a helpless character.

With enough time and creativity, a couple of years later, I was able to stockpile my resources—financial and emotional—and afford two bedrooms for my little family. Two bedrooms meant more than just extra space. It meant that I wasn't stuck anymore. I went from sleeping on the floor next to my kids' beds to having a mattress, then to having a bed, and finally to having my very own bedroom. I was moving forward. I allowed myself to fall in love again. I built a career that gave me purpose. I watched my children thrive.

Ten years after my life had ground to a halt, I found myself sitting in a fancy-schmancy building across the table from fancy-schmancy people. It was the type of meeting I actually shaved my armpits for (like, both of them) and for once wore a blouse not yet baptized by fluids harboring my children's DNA. The fancy people praised me for the videos and posts I'd been sharing online for a few years and they admired my large social media following. They thought I was successful enough that they wanted to offer me something more. "So, Kristina, what do you ultimately want? A television show? A speaking tour? What do you want to do with your life?"

Without any thought, I blurted out: "I want to be for others what I needed when I was at my lowest." As I spoke, I could feel my voice catching in my throat.

I'd never said those words aloud before, or even thought of them specifically. Yet there was my mission, as clear as day. The answer to why I had fought through everything. The answer to what made me get off that floor and live again. The reason why I felt such a strong pull to share my story, my humor, my hope.

Every human I've ever met is broken. Every parent I've ever met struggles. We all feel regrets; we're wounded by our failures, hobbled by our insecurities. When you're in the midst of the worst of it, the darkness feels permanent. But it's not. It is possible to find meaning and value and connection and humor in your life right now—in your relationships with your kids, your friends, your spouse, and yourself. It is possible to stop feeling defeated and stuck. Hold on for dear life and do not give up. But don't hold still and be passive; don't go numb to the good happening all around you, even when life is at its messiest. You do not need to be transformed by the latest twenty-seven-step program. You do not need to take pointers from that mom who seems to have it all figured out. (FYI, she doesn't. No one does.) You don't need to aspire to more—more money, more stuff, or more answers. You just need to show up. Just as you are. Flawed and unshowered or perfectly polished. Just as you are.

No matter what you're facing, failure never has to be the end of a sentence. You can always put a nice bold comma on that disaster, take a breath, and continue right on. Hold on, but don't hold still. Keep turning the pages of your story until you reach an easier chapter, and you just might end up somewhere better than where you started. With a fresh, unexpired Starbucks pastry. And enough hope to spare.

Hold On,
But Don't Hold Still

One

Wish Out Loud

There's a moment at most kids' birthday parties, just after the "Happy Birthday" song has been sung, when the birthday kid takes a big breath and gets ready to blow out the candles on their cake. "Make a wish!" the parents say. "But don't tell anyone what it is. If you tell, it won't come true!"

I hate this moment.

We're supposed to have big dreams and wild ambitions—for family, career, success, recognition—yet we're taught from birthday number one that saying what we want out loud is a bad idea. It's a jinx. It's embarrassing.

No matter what your aspirations are, whether you want to write a bestselling novel, host a talk show, or run the country, they'll never happen if you don't try. But it's hard to muster up the confidence to try without your loved ones cheering you on, and they're not even going to get the chance to support you if you never let them know what your dreams are.

That's why I do the birthday cake thing a little differently with my kids. At candle time, I scream, "Make a wish! Say it out loud! Yell it at the top of your lungs!" And then we all cheer for each other's biggest dreams and do what we can to make sure they come true for one another.

My hope is to give my kids the confidence to dream out loud. I want to show them that ridiculously good things *do* happen, even if they seem completely unbelievable. I mean, that's exactly what happened to me.

When my second husband, Philip, and I got married, we couldn't afford a honeymoon. I was still waiting tables, and he had decided to change careers and go back to school to become a CPA. (Because, apparently, there are people in this world who actually enjoy doing taxes. And math.) We were living in a small, run-down apartment in Alhambra, California, with my six-year-old son, Luka, and four-year-old daughter, Matea. To get to our front door, you'd first have to walk by a rusting, claw-foot bathtub that our landlord, a sweet old man named Will who lived upstairs in the building's only other unit, intended to turn into a fountain but never quite got around to finishing. (Honestly, I could see potential in his vision and would have loved a cheerful water fixture on my front lawn. Unfortunately, the reality is that it was just a tetanus hazard filled with what looked like poop water.) The first time I tried to open the oven door in our kitchen, the handle fell off. The washer and dryer were also crammed into the kitchen alongside the worn-out stove. But Philip and I were just so happy to have a washer and dryer at all. We were a very typical young family: we didn't have all the resources we dreamed of, but we had a surplus of love.

A few days after our wedding, I was running around our apartment as usual, doing, doing, doing, knowing I'd still probably finish the day asking myself, *How did I get nothing done today when I did so many things?* (answer: motherhood!), when Philip startled me with a question.

"What do you want to do? I mean, besides being a mother?"

"What do you mean?"

"You have all this creativity and all this passion. Is there anything else you'd want to do with it?"

"Like get a job other than waiting tables?"

"It doesn't have to be a new job. It can be a hobby. Either one. Just something where you can use your gifts."

I stared at him blankly for a few moments. Being a mother of young children means you spend a lot of your energy thinking about what other people need. You're always wiping something for somebody or cutting something for somebody. When you finally make your way to the soothing blank bottom of an empty sink, it's almost inevitable that you'll blink and the sink will be full again. It's like some reverse *Sorcerer's Apprentice* trick, only instead of having the soaring beauty of the Philadelphia Orchestra as backup, your soundtrack is provided by toddlers banging away with wooden spoons on pots and pans. Just a few years earlier, I'd been going through a painful divorce while struggling to provide for my two young children as a broke single mom. I had been trying to keep my head above water for so long that survival mode was my default. I hadn't stopped to consider my dreams or desires, independent of my children's well-being. Philip's question genuinely caught me off guard.

"I have no idea. I really don't know."

This realization made me a bit emotional. I used to have dreams and creative ambitions. How was I suddenly this lost?

Philip handed me his car keys. "I'll take care of dinner and get the kids to bed. You just go. Go somewhere where you can think. Get away from the distractions of parenting and think about what you would have wanted to do if life hadn't gotten so hard."

I drove around the suburbs of Los Angeles—not really headed anywhere, just thinking. Sometimes you need to get away from the noise in order to hear your heart speak.

A few hours later, I returned home with a gas tank on empty and my mind on full blast. "I want to do something with cooking!" I said as I charged back into the apartment, out of breath from excitement. "Philip, I think I've got it! When I was at my lowest, cooking is what made me feel alive. Being able to feed people made me feel like I had something to offer when I had almost nothing. I'm thinking maybe I could start a website where I post my recipes. And, I don't know how we could make this happen, but maybe we could figure out a way to film some cooking videos? Something really fun, different from what's out there. I want to make the people who are watching feel empowered. I want to make other moms laugh and maybe even give them a little hope that their life and their kitchen and their cooking skills don't have to be perfect. None of it has to be perfect to still be really good."

"This is awesome! How can I help?" Philip pulled me in for a hug.

See that response? That's the response we all deserve when we articulate a new dream. We all need a Philip.

I spent the next seven months revisiting all of my favorite

recipes. I had learned to cook from my grandmother, who never measured anything, and so neither did I. But now I had to start measuring out every single thing in order to write down all of my recipes in a way anyone could follow. My goal was to launch my website on my birthday (April 26) with exactly seventy-nine recipes (because I was born in 1979).

Philip saved up money and surprised me with a laptop so I could start building my site. He was juggling his grad school classes, helping with the kids, and running to the grocery store (sometimes four or five times in one day) so that I could keep refining my recipes. He was also solving the daily technical issues that kept popping up and also kicking my ass in the most loving way every time I thought about giving up. Jo, my best friend, who lives in Rhode Island, spent hours editing my recipes to make sure everything was grammatically correct. With four kids of her own, I'm not sure how she found the time, but she was rooting for me and so excited to see my passion lit up in this way.

As the end of April neared, I had to cook two or three meals at a time to hit my birthday deadline, and therefore completely misrepresented the culinary standards my husband and children should expect from me. Don't care for Thai? No problem, we also have Italian and French options on our menu this evening! I sent my children to school with warm lunches every day that spring like some kind of Martha Stewart protégé, and then disappointed them terribly when things eventually returned to normal PB&J fare. Thankfully, our friends were more than happy to come over to be our taste testers and help us chow down on the vast quantities of food coming out of my kitchen. Our landlord, who lived alone and was either 92 or 101, depending on which day you asked him, was the happy recipient of many of the meals I was working on, too.

The recipes were coming together, but I still really wanted to make a few videos to accompany them and wasn't quite sure where to start. I didn't own a good camera, I didn't own a smartphone, and even if I had, I knew nothing about filming or editing. Philip made some phone calls, and through his brothers, I was introduced to a character named Brian Hardin.

Brian is a tall, laid-back hippie who cares about health and nutrition the way I care about donuts and butter. He's creative and eccentric and funny. He always has a big smile on his face and regularly serves his guests sugar-free chia cake in an apartment covered with wall tapestries, mandalas, and peace signs. Brian also has a lot of experience filming and editing, and had already worked on a few documentaries and music videos when I met him. We hit it off immediately.

We mapped out six videos, which he charged me next to nothing for, because, as Brian said, "Philip's brothers are like family to me, so you're family now, too!" I maintain that he was also secretly excited to be force-fed bites of all the cheesy, gooey, chocolatey, bacon-filled recipes we'd be filming. Since we were ambitious, short on time, and completely nuts, we decided to shoot all six videos in one delicious, messy day.

I spent the next few weeks going to Brian's apartment, often with Luka and Matea in tow. While he and I worked long days editing the hours of raw footage into short, frazzled-mom-friendly three-minute videos, the kids wreaked havoc on Brian's ashram-like living space. Brian didn't try to control the projects or direct too much. He saw that his job was to do what he could to bring out the best in me. He not only indulged my crazy, wacky sense of humor but encouraged it, and through his editing, he made me shine. Brian did this brilliant thing where he would tell me he'd cut but would actually keep rolling so he could capture me dancing to made-up songs and being my goofy self, and that often wound up being the best footage.

The very first video we filmed and edited opens with me standing in a friend's kitchen—the richest friend I knew at the time with the most expensive-looking kitchen. The audience sees me in this gorgeous home, talking about my perfect life. Then, suddenly, an elegant woman walks in and reveals that I don't actually live there, I'm just someone she hired to clean her house. From that, we cut to my real kitchen: small and old and messy. No granite countertops, no recessed lighting, just a wonky oven and a stained sink overflowing with dishes. And there I was, proudly showing off my very flawed but wonderful home. The entire point of that first video was to set the tone for my approach to cooking and to life: you don't have to be perfect or rich or fancy to thrive. Even more than my grandmother's three-cheese Croatian strudel, this message is what I most wanted to share with other parents.

Finally, on April 26, 2010, my thirty-first birthday, I launched my first blog, *Sticky Cook*. The name came from the idea that everything in my life was sticky. My finances were sticky, my divorce was sticky, my relationships with family and my ex were sticky, my children are sticky (because children, for some reason, even seconds after washing their hands, are always sticky), and my favorite foods are sticky, too. I also loved the idea of using a word that might have a negative connotation and turning it into a positive. My tagline read "Life is sticky . . . Dig in!" Instead of trying to make life seem flawless, I wanted people to embrace the mess and the chaos and still create something delicious from it.

As soon as *Sticky Cook* went live, I started receiving supportive phone calls and messages from friends. I was so proud to have seen this project through, and so grateful for Brian and Philip and Jo and everyone who'd come together to help me make this dream a reality by my birthday deadline. It felt so good to celebrate this milestone with friends who'd been cheering me on every step of the way. There were even a few people with no prior connection to me at all who came across my videos or recipes and shared them online. I was thrilled. When I blew out the candles on my cake that night, I wished that this new adventure would thrive. And I wished it out loud.

Just nine days after launching the site, I received an unexpected email from a complete stranger named Kim Schofield. Kim got straight to the point, telling me that she'd seen my videos and thought I should enter *Oprah's Search for the Next TV Star* because I belonged on TV. Not only did I not know Kim, Philip and I didn't even own a working television, so we didn't know about Oprah's competition.

Even though Kim didn't know anything about me beyond my few silly videos, she was quick to answer all of my questions and encouraged me as if she had known me for years. She wasn't a producer or involved in the entertainment industry in any way. Kim was just a warm, middle-aged mom from Arizona who connected with my message so strongly that she felt compelled to write to me. Somehow, through the power of putting myself out there and the magic of the internet, I'd found an advocate. Or rather, she'd found me.

From Kim, I learned that Oprah was running the competition to promote the launch of her new network, OWN (Oprah Winfrey Network), and anyone could submit a video pitching their own TV show to her. Ten people would be chosen to be contestants on a reality show competition produced by Mark Burnett, an award-winning producer who had created shows like *Survivor*, *Shark Tank*, and *The Apprentice*. Each week, one entrant would be eliminated, and the final winner would actually get to make their own television show for the Oprah Winfrey Network. Entering required a three-minute audition video. By the time I learned about the competition, the deadline was only a few days away and more than ten thousand auditions had already been submitted.

"What do you think, Philip? Should I even bother?"

"Bother?!? Are you kidding? You're perfect for this!"

We scheduled a time with Brian to cut together some of the footage we already had into an audition video. When I clicked the submit button, there was a small part of me that actually hoped that maybe, just maybe, a producer would notice me and at least call me in for a meeting. But that hope quickly faded. I spent the entire night watching audition videos on Oprah's website. Some of them featured real news anchors or former child actors I immediately recognized, some were so moving that they made me cry, others looked like they had been put together by a professional television producer, and some even had special effects. My video seemed very amateurish by comparison. By the time submissions closed, more than fifteen thousand auditions had been entered.

A couple of weeks after entering the competition, I was on my way to meet a friend for a late lunch in Pasadena when my phone rang with an unknown number. I let it go to voice mail, but then I worried that maybe the phone call was from someone at my kids' school and that one of my children might have come down with Ebola or decided it was a really great idea to drink a bunch of hand sanitizer, so I pulled over on a side street to listen to the message.

"Hi. I'm a casting producer for Mark Burnett Productions. We love your video! Please call me back as soon as you can."

This couldn't be real. I called Philip and asked him to look up the guy's name. "See if you can find anything on him. Does he really work for Mark Burnett? This is probably just a prank call from a friend who knows I sent in a video." Philip quickly confirmed that the guy calling did in fact work for Mark Burnett. I texted my friend: Gonna be late. Then I took a deep breath and, with my hands and my voice shaking, called the guy back.

You know that feeling from before cell phones and caller ID when the landline would ring and your heart would stop for a small eternity because the person who answered might be that boy you really liked from school? (If you're a parent reading this book, you're probably old enough to know that feeling. Congratulations, our kids already think we're dinosaurs.) Well, that's what making this call felt like. The production company had probably made a mistake and called the wrong Kristina. This was going to be an awkward conversation.

But they hadn't made a mistake. When the casting producer picked up, he said, "Oh my God, Kristina, I just watched your tape multiple times and we're all cracking up in here. Your video is one of my favorites! I don't want to get your hopes up, but I'm gonna be shocked if you don't make it to the next level." I could barely think straight as he walked me through the paperwork I'd have to fill out to move forward in the competition. By the end of the call, I felt like the air around my entire body was buzzing. Did this just happen?

The next few months were even more surreal. I kept advancing further and further in the competition, until eventually I found myself in a hotel near LAX with the other top forty entrants, waiting to be interviewed by Mark Burnett himself. At first, I was a pile of nerves. But I'd done a lot of theater work back in grade school and college, and I found that if I pretended I was walking onto a stage every time I walked into a meeting room, things didn't feel so scary. After all, I'd forgotten lines in plays before and improvised, and the shows had gone on without a hitch. If what had caught these producers' attention was my video, where, thanks to Brian, I was shown being completely myself, then I just needed to continue being completely myself. Nothing more.

Somehow, it worked. Out of the remaining competitors, Oprah handpicked me, along with nine others, to compete on her reality show. I don't remember my exact reaction when I received that phone call from the casting producer. All I can remember thinking was, *OPRAH KNOWS WHO I AM*. She would recognize my face in a lineup! If someone mentioned *my* name to *her*, she'd casually reply, "Oh, yeah. I know who that is." The real competition was about to begin, but I already felt like I had won more than I ever expected to win in my life.

Just a few years earlier I'd been so broke I had to borrow money from a friend to buy myself a box of tampons. I had been sure I was going to be alone, poor, and miserable forever. There were people in my life who were close to me who believed I'd never amount to anything, and I believed it also. I was certain I was always going to be someone others looked down on, someone people pitied. Fighting my way through that dark place and meeting and marrying Philip already felt like I'd stumbled onto more than my fair share of good fortune. I had a wonderful husband. My kids were healthy. What more could I ask for?

When I entered that competition, I wasn't looking to have a TV show, not really. What I wanted, what I needed more than anything, was for someone to look at this new little dream I had poured hours and sweat and tears into and tell me that it was worth dreaming out loud, that I did have something worthwhile to offer to the world. Now here I was in the top ten of *Oprah's Search for the Next TV Star*. I knew that I'd never win the contest and I didn't need to. I was beyond grateful and thrilled to be validated by the most powerful person in television.

But my glamorous validation also came with complications. Participating in the reality show competition with the top ten meant that I was now living in a hotel in Los Angeles. Depending on how far along I made it on the show, I would be away from my family for one week to seven weeks. No visits. Only one fifteen-minute phone call home every Friday. I was a year into my marriage with Philip, and he was about to be a single dad to my two young kids, without any way to reach me directly. Initially, when I learned about this, I balked. No way was I going to leave my kids for that long. But Philip wouldn't let me withdraw. "The kids and I will be great. I've got this. You've come so far, you have to keep going!" So I went.

I quit my waitressing job without being allowed to tell anyone the truth about why I was leaving. I had signed a $5 million non-disclosure agreement and no one was allowed to know I was one of the ten contestants—not my coworkers, not my friends, not my kids.

The morning before I left, I filmed a few video messages for Luka and Matea. I wanted Philip to show them a video of me talking to them every few days because I knew this would be a big transition for them. Thankfully, they were already well bonded to Philip and considered him a second dad.

As I was packing the final few things in my suitcase, Philip said to me, "You're going to win this."

If you want to know the type of guy my husband is, all you have to know is that in fifth grade he was running for student council and his best friend was running against him. Philip lost that election by one vote, *his* vote, which he cast for his best friend. Philip is the type of guy who will always set you up to win. He roots for people in his life so genuinely that you can't help but start rooting for yourself.

I did end up spending the next seven weeks living in a hotel room. While that might seem like an orgasmic fantasy to most exhausted, overworked moms of young children, the hotel room got lonely quickly. I had no phone, no computer, no television. The production team even took the magazines and newspapers out of our rooms. The contestants weren't allowed to talk to one another at all unless we were on camera, because the producers didn't want to run the risk that their viewers might miss out on any good drama. We weren't even allowed to ride in the same elevator together or eat meals without our "babysitters" (as I called them) watching our every move. I would have turned one of my pillows into a companion like Wilson the volleyball was for Tom Hanks in *Cast Away* if they'd just given me a Sharpie.

Though I missed Philip and the kids immensely, I loved getting a crash course in television production and hosting. I got to do segments with Dr. Phil, Gayle King, Vera Wang, Suze Orman, Arsenio Hall, and Curtis Stone, who taught me how to make a prosciutto-wrapped pork dish that I still whip up. But most important, I got to meet Oprah face-to-face. O-P-R-A-H. *Oprah.* Oprah? OPRAH FREAKIN' WINFREY!

She was everything I hoped she would be but didn't really expect she could be. As powerful and famous as she is, she was still so . . . normal. Warm and friendly, self-deprecating and hilarious. Within seconds of being introduced, she was immediately meeting me on my level and putting me at ease.

"Are you one of those people who follows recipes?" she asked.

"I'm one of those people who opens her cabinets and says to herself, 'What magic can I make out of this?'"

"Oh, me, too! Can you teach anyone how to cook? Do you think you could teach Gayle, who raised her kids on SpaghettiOs, how to cook?"

Right there. See that? I'm sitting across from Oprah Winfrey, media mogul, and we're talking about SpaghettiOs.

I believe the reason Oprah is so successful is because of her remarkable ability to make you feel like every word you say, every opinion you have, truly matters. She genuinely wants to hear you. I remember making a mental note as I sat across from her: *Kristina, make sure you do this for people in your life, especially your children.* It's so easy to be distracted and dismissive. But thanks to

Oprah, I gave myself a new challenge: Can I make sure that my children walk away from every conversation they have with me feeling that they were truly heard and that what they have to say genuinely matters to me? I'm not always successful at this, but— like I always say—every day is a second chance to suck at life a little less.

At the end of the seven most surreal weeks of my life, the competition came down to my favorite fellow contestant, Zach Anner, and . . . me. I couldn't fully understand how I'd made it so far, and I especially didn't understand how anyone could consider me to be on the same level of talent as Zach. Not only was he funny and charming on camera, he was also the sweetest, most gracious, thoughtful person off camera. I could tell that about him without ever having been allowed a full conversation with him when the cameras weren't rolling.

From the start, Zach was the cool, funny one all the other contestants wanted to meet. We'd all seen his audition tape, which had been an overnight viral internet sensation. In it he explained how he had "cerebral palsy, the sexiest of the palsies . . ." and that he wanted to make a travel show "for people who never thought they could travel." Throughout the competition, Zach impressed everyone with his quick wit and humor, and I was genuinely thrilled he'd made it to the final round. Even though Zach and I were on opposing teams, we'd been rooting for each other the entire time. There's not much similarity between us on the surface. He's this single guy and I'm a divorced/remarried mom of two. But I recognized his grit and his spirit. Our struggles weren't the same, but neither of us had had an easy or typical life, and I felt a connection with him.

The day before the finale, we begged the producers to allow us to have breakfast together. We waited as they talked to their bosses and their bosses talked to the network execs, as if they were coordinating Middle East peace talks. Back and forth the negotiations went, with Zach and me promising the producers that we wouldn't discuss the show or other contestants or tangle in any drama. We just wanted to get to know each other better and talk the way normal, non-reality-show-restricted people talk.

Finally, we were given the green light, and over waffles and bacon, Zach and I hit it off as if we had known each other our entire lives. We shared some strengths and insecurities, and also a sugar addiction. We both thought of ourselves as underdogs and I think we were probably the only two contestants who genuinely didn't expect to have a chance to win.

I left that breakfast desperately hoping Zach would win. The producers kept asking me to say something bad about him to ramp up the drama of the finale, but I wouldn't do it. I wanted him to win and I said so. "If you don't say you want to win, Oprah's going to think you don't really want this. You're going to come off as someone who won't work hard and isn't a fighter." I learned later that they'd baited Zach the exact same way, and he didn't bite either! We were casting our ballots for each other. At this point we were not only dreaming out loud for ourselves, we were dreaming out loud for each other.

A few hours after our breakfast, Zach and I were under the spotlight again, back on the set of the reality competition. Sitting on opposite sides of the stage with numerous cameras pointed at us, we waited to find out who would take home the final prize: a television show, one hundred thousand dollars, and a brand-new Chevy Equinox. As we nervously sat in our seats, occasionally throwing supportive glances at each other, Oprah said, "Big moments should always be shared with those closest to us." Then out onto the set walked Philip, and Zach's mom.

There was nothing Oprah could have unveiled that would have made me happier than seeing my husband's face. To be there, on that stage, at the peak of two emotionally grueling months, closer than I ever could have imagined I would be to realizing a dream bigger than any I'd even dared to dream, and to be able to share that moment with the man who'd first encouraged me to say my dream out loud, was the most magical, Oprah-esque thing Oprah could have done. Except for what she did next—she declared *both* Zach and me the winners!

I cried. I cried because I finally believed that my dreams were worth pursuing. I cried because I was standing next to a man who'd always believed that. And I cried because now I had *Oprah* believing in me, too. And to top it all off, I didn't have to cut my biggest competitor down in order to reach the top. There was room for both of us. There is always room for more than one person to thrive, and pursuing one's dreams should never feel like a rivalry.

Just two hours later, I was finally reunited with my kids in our little apartment. But I still couldn't tell them about this huge, life-changing thing that had happened to me. If they'd been the ages they are now, I would have told them, but I was legally obligated to keep the secret for another *four* months, until the finale of the show aired on TV, and they were so little that I couldn't risk one of them saying something at school. Plus my daughter,

Matea, came bouncing up to me with her own exciting news. "Mommy, Mommy! I just lost a tooth!" As usual, my children helped put everything back into perspective.

For someone who considers blabbing her greatest gift, it was both mentally and physically painful to keep this secret. And I may or may not have told a few people I wasn't supposed to tell, but I'll confirm that with you after I double-check the expiration date on that thousand-page, single-spaced $5 million nondisclosure agreement.

During this time, Zach was the one person who understood exactly what I had been through, and having him to process all these new emotions with was such a gift, and I was more grateful than ever that we won together. I don't think my brain or heart would have had the capacity to process it all alone. When you're keeping a secret that big, four months feels like an eternity, and you start to wonder, "Did that *actually* happen?" If you don't talk about something with the people in your life, it doesn't feel real. Which is just another reason you should always say anything you dream or plan out loud.

Even though holding in the news was excruciating, there was a lot to contemplate and to be excited about. A month after winning, the original top ten contestants were invited to appear on the very last season of the legendary *Oprah Winfrey Show*.

I had watched Oprah's talk show all through my teens and twenties, and on an episode of *Oprah*, I first heard the idea that not loving every moment of motherhood is normal and does not make anybody (ahem, me) a bad mom. That stuck with me and made the hard moments of mothering so much more bearable. *The Oprah Winfrey Show* is also where I first heard Dr. Phil say that it's better for kids to come from a broken home than to live in a broken home, a statement that I felt gave me the permission I needed to leave when my first marriage was falling apart. I received so many powerful takeaways from Oprah's show (including the importance of checking my poop shape . . . thanks, Dr. Oz!), and I couldn't believe that just a few years after hitting my lowest point, a point where I had felt completely unlovable and worthless, I'd now be walking onto the *Oprah* stage as a guest, standing next to her and keeping the secret that the world's most famous talk-show host was about to be my boss.

During my one-on-one interview with Oprah back during the reality competition, she asked me, "Whether you are awarded your own show or not, what will you take away from this experience?"

I remember trying really hard not to get emotional as I answered, "I think I'm a lot better at finally shutting down the lies that I believed about what I'm capable of or what I deserve in life. So I leave with a whole new motivation and excitement to go do what I know I am destined to do, and to not let anyone else tell me I can't."

Oprah smiled and said, "That is perfection."

And it is.

Two

Hot Dogs with Oprah

S o, I was standing in a parking lot, eating hot dogs with Oprah.

I feel like I should repeat that sentence because certain mind-boggling parts of life deserve repeating: I was standing in a parking lot, eating hot dogs with Oprah.

The entire crew of the reality show I'd just won had moved from the studio out into a large parking lot where the famous LA hot-dog joint Pink's was catering an after-party for all of us.

Philip and I were chatting with Oprah, pretending all of this was totally normal. In between bites of hot dog, with Oprah (had to throw that in one more time), she asked us how we planned on celebrating this win.

"I'm really craving buffalo chicken fingers from Applebee's," I replied, trying not to drip mustard on my chest. I gave Philip an excited look. "I'm pretty sure they're half off during happy hour!"

Oprah laughed. I think she was expecting a fancier answer.

"Stay this way, Kristina." She grabbed me by the shoulders while I tried not to pee myself from excitement that Oprah was touching me. "Listen. People, especially in this industry, will try to change you, but I love how you don't pretend you're something you're not. You bring your light by completely embracing who you are. Stay this way."

Through my interactions with Oprah, I loved how genuine and passionate and down-to-earth she was. She was also a great hugger. Philip got one of those great Oprah hugs as we said goodbye to her that day, and later, when friends would ask him what it was like to hug Oprah, he would say, "It's like taking a warm, soothing bath." And that is *exactly* what it's like!

A few months later, after the finale aired and the world finally knew Zach and I had won, the time came to start preproduction on my cooking show. After those long months holding in the secret that I'd won the competition, I was so excited to finally get to work!

I knew Oprah was busy with the launch of her network and numerous other projects, so I never expected her to be directly involved with my series. But when I entered my first big production meeting armed with a thick three-ring binder I'd filled with ideas and recipes, I didn't see a single familiar face. We gathered in a formal conference room around a cartoonishly large wooden table, with more chairs than anyone could ever need, and pitchers of water just far enough away that it would be awkward to reach over and pour yourself a glass. I took a seat at one end of the table and the production team filtered in and settled themselves together at the other. By the end of that meeting, I felt like we were just as far apart creatively. The production team had to please the network. The network, being in its first year, was still trying to find its footing. And I was left trying to figure out how much say I actually had to make my show what I felt it should be.

As I had with my online videos, I wanted to create a cooking show that wasn't intimidating and was unlike any cooking show I'd ever seen. I originally wanted to call it *Sticky Cook* after my blog, but that quickly got shut down, so we went with my second choice: *Kristina's Fearless Kitchen*. The ideas I had were not the norm for a cooking show, because the norm doesn't make parents feel normal. It leaves them feeling inadequate. I wanted to do more than share my favorite recipes with a larger audience. I wanted to reach every struggling mom and let her know that she's okay, that real life is messy and chaotic and unpredictable, and that none of that is actually a bad thing.

I proposed an episode where my kid is throwing a massive tantrum while I'm trying to cook. That idea got shot down. I proposed an episode where I'm roasting a chicken but get distracted by the unrelenting demands of motherhood and burn the whole dish, so the episode ends with my ordering pizza for my family for dinner. That idea got shot down. I proposed an episode where I make breakfast wearing mismatched pajamas with day-old mascara smeared under my eyes and a crayon stuck in my messy hair, all while drinking coffee straight out of a coffeepot. That idea got shot down, too.

As each idea was rejected, my newfound confidence shrank. These were professionals who'd worked in television for years. If they said something "just wouldn't work" for TV or "that's not how it's done" or "our research shows that your target audience wouldn't respond well to that," who was I to disagree?

It's funny the lessons we have to learn over and over again. My experience with Oprah during the competition had been a revelation about my own self-worth. I wanted so badly to put my foot down and stick up for my own ideas. But when you've spent most of your life believing your voice doesn't matter, it's easy to slide back into that familiar way of thinking about yourself and your place in the world.

When I'd walked into the casting interview with Mark Burnett, I didn't have anything to lose and nobody to let down but myself. But now there was a lot at stake and many people I could let down. Studio executives had invested money in me. Oprah believed in me. These producers were investing their time and energy in *me*. I didn't want to disappoint anyone. So I didn't fight back on much as the professionals laid out their vision for the show. I nodded in agreement to ideas they loved and I hated, and ended up with a completely different show than what I had imagined.

During the production process, *Kristina's Fearless Kitchen* became *The Ambush Cook*. I hated that title, but it didn't seem to matter. Each episode, I ambushed someone—a mom at a fast-food restaurant buying takeout for her kids, a bachelor who used only the microwave in his kitchen, a woman who was eight months pregnant and didn't know anything about cooking—and dragged them back to "my kitchen" and taught them how to make something from scratch.

In the *Sticky Cook* videos I'd made with Brian, my tone aimed to disrupt the hierarchal dynamic of most cooking shows: I'm struggling, you're struggling, and maybe together we can muddle our way through this crazy thing called parenthood. But in

The Ambush Cook, I was presented as the expert and each episode's guest as my incompetent student. I cooked with perfect technique in a pristine kitchen and never, ever messed up. I felt like a fraud.

A few weeks after the last episode of the first season aired, I got a phone call from the network saying they would not be renewing the show. It felt like getting dumped by a guy I knew wasn't really right for me anyway. It hurts not to be wanted, but I knew my show wasn't lifting any moms out of their slump. I was more upset by what could've been—by the opportunity I'd let slip through my fingers—than I was about the cancellation.

After my cooking show ended, several other networks reached out to me. I kept flying to New York to talk with interested executives and even got signed for a few different cooking and parenting shows, only to have it all fall apart every single time. And every single time, I felt like there was no one to blame but myself.

I would walk into these meetings with major networks and they would respond to my passion. But their final feedback always added up to some variation of "We love you! We love your personality and your passion. But we just don't know what that show is. Would you be willing to change [insert long list of personality traits they didn't like or credentials they'd need me to pretend to have]?" I didn't fit the mold. Everybody needed me to be some sort of expert. Nobody wanted me just as I was.

Once you've eaten hot dogs with Oprah, you expect your life to be different. You don't think you'll still be stuck in a small apartment, unemployed. But I wasn't willing to pretend to be something I wasn't just to be on television. Compromising my genuine self was a betrayal of the girl who took years to embrace her vivacious personality, who struggled and overcame, who was trying, by example, to teach her own children how much freedom, joy, and power come from being completely authentic.

So I decided to put my career dreams away and expand our family, something Philip and I had talked about since getting married. It's not that I didn't care that the dream I'd wished for hadn't turned out the way I'd hoped. I wasn't totally at peace with it. But I had tried, really tried, and it hadn't worked out. It was a huge disappointment, but it wasn't my whole world. The best part of my life, my favorite story, my favorite chapter, has always been motherhood. I wanted more children, and two years later, Philip, Matea, Luka, and I welcomed Ari into our family.

When Ari was two months old, we moved out of our little apartment and into a house we had been saving for. Ari got to have an actual bedroom instead of the closet-turned-nursery he'd had at the apartment. My whole world became about taking care of my new little guy, getting my older two kids transitioned to a new town and a new school system, and settling us into our new home.

One night when everyone in the house was asleep except for Ari and me, I sat down on the couch in the living room to breast-feed him. Ari was about eleven months old and I was starting to wean him. I knew he was my last baby, so my breastfeeding career was coming to an end. As I looked down at him, my glance shifted from his cute little face to my busted stomach. It was covered in stretch marks.

They say those suckers are genetic, but they are freakin' liars. My mother had three children and not a single stretch mark. I had three children and my stomach looked like a relief map of Disaster City. But as I was staring at my stomach with annoyance, it suddenly hit me: my body is feeding another human being. Right now, in this moment, there is actual legit milk dripping from my chest into my baby's mouth, nourishing and growing my child, whom *I* nourished and grew in that body. And yet here I am, instead of enjoying this unbelievably beautiful and magical moment that will soon end forever, complaining to myself about something shallow and unimportant.

And then I wondered: how many other moms are missing out on an incredible moment with their kid because they're distracted by self-judgment?

The following morning, I unpacked the camera Zach Anner and his brother had given me when Ari was born. They had come to the hospital to meet him and pushed the camera into my hands. "You should be making videos! And since you haven't made any since your *Sticky Cook* ones, here's a camera to guilt you into it. Now that we spent money on it, you'd be a really bad friend if you don't use it."

For eleven months, that camera sat in a box, unopened. But the morning after I realized how magical my nipples are, I unwrapped it, googled how to use it, and filmed my first parenting video: "4 Reasons Stretch Marks Are Sexy."

In the video, I argue that stretch marks are scars, and scars are sexy. (I mean, come on. Joaquin Phoenix. Seal. Jason Momoa! . . . Harry Potter?) If a guy gets into a brawl at a bar, beats some dude up, and leaves with a scar, he will tell that dumb story to his buddies over and over again and show off that scar like it's a badge of honor.

I also point out that stretch marks are like tattoos. I personally have lightning strikes, tiger stripes, and the entire map of Italy along my midriff. In a tattoo parlor, these would have cost me hundreds of dollars, but mine were free! (And my husband, an accountant, likes to remind me that saving money is very sexy.)

And how did I get my scars? Not from punching someone, not from gritting my teeth in a tattoo parlor, but from giving someone *life*. I made people! Like with real organs and stuff. What has some dude made lately? A sandwich? And did it have a pulse?

Throughout the video I show off my stretch marks, hoping that anyone else who might be judging their body would find a little humor and encouragement in my silliness. When I finally finished battling iMovie (because anything technical always feels like a personal attack on my brain) and uploaded the stretch mark video onto YouTube, I felt excited in a way that I hadn't felt since I'd launched *Sticky Cook*. It was great to be doing something creative again, and I knew that no matter how many people my video reached, I was putting something good out into the world, a message that was meant to help people and make them laugh.

Almost immediately after it went live, I started hearing from moms. Their positive feedback motivated me to make another video. And then another one. I was pulling all-nighters like I was back in college. I made every mistake you could possibly make (and a few that I'm pretty sure no one else has ever made) figuring out how to film myself and edit the videos. I'd have to reshoot things because the image was blurry or the volume was off or I'd left the lens cap on. Once, inexplicably, all the footage came out red like someone had bled all over the screen. More than once, after spending many hours editing, I accidentally deleted the project file and had to start all over from scratch. But as frustrating as the mechanics were, I was exhilarated by this creative outlet. Every time a parent commented that one of my videos made them laugh or encouraged them, I received a jolt of inspiration.

The fourth parenting video I made was snarky, aimed at shutting down any arguments against breastfeeding in public. I had to rerecord it four separate times because of technical issues (read: technical incompetence). A few days after posting it, I was trying to get some of Ari's breakfast out of my hair when my phone started blowing up with texts from friends letting me know that Ashton Kutcher had shared my video on his Facebook page. I don't know how he'd stumbled onto it, but he posted it on his social media pages and wrote, "Sometimes sarcasm is the best way to combat ignorance." Suddenly, people were sharing the video all over the internet and it was quickly going viral. I remember Philip and me lying in bed late one night, refreshing the screen over and over again as the counter neared and finally reached a million views. A million views! People had watched something I'd made a MILLION times! That was probably more than the views on all the episodes of *The Ambush Cook* combined.

The next day, Philip took me out to a fancy restaurant. "This needs to be celebrated. You put yourself out there. You won this huge thing, and then when that didn't work out, you had the courage to get back up and do it again your own way."

My hobby turned into my career. I loved being in complete control of the content I was creating and not having anybody try to make me an expert or suggest I "tone it down a bit." A lot of people seemed completely okay with me just being me. Finally.

. . .

WHAT WE'RE TOLD about ourselves as children follows us into adulthood. As a little girl, I was told I was too talkative, too loud, too hyper, too impulsive, too candid, too, too, too, too . . . *much*. I asked too many questions, cried too much when I heard a sad story, felt too much enthusiasm about everything. And so I grew up and became an adult who was too much. Being told you're too much can often leave you feeling like you're not enough. Weird how that works, right?

What I tell my kids, through my words and actions, about who they are really matters. This is both scary and empowering. Even in those crazy mom moments when I find a part of their personalities or their quirks annoying, I need to be careful how I respond to them. I am one of the most powerful, influential people in their lives, whether I want that power or not. They will remember and carry the words I say for a very long time. And they will believe them.

My first son, Luka, is the loud, hyper, talkative type (it's genetic), and sometimes I had to bite my tongue to avoid criticizing him for or defining him by the same personality traits I struggled with, and to instead give him an appropriate outlet. I want my children to be respectful, but I also want to encourage them to become their most authentic selves. So when we had people coming over for dinner, instead of giving Luka the impression that children should be seen and not heard, I would ask him to prepare some fun questions for our guests. That way, the conversation he started was about other people, but it also gave Luka's outgoing, funny personality a chance to shine.

For a while I described my daughter, Matea, as "the shy and reserved one." Her kindergarten teacher told me that she couldn't even get her to raise her hand in class. But telling her—and others—that she was shy didn't help her confidence grow, so I made a conscious effort to stop labeling her and to pay attention to *all* of the ways my child would show me who she was. To my surprise, once the label was off, she started doing theater in school and now she's a teenager who is comfortable onstage in front of hundreds of people.

It's easy for us adults, once we decide to become parents, to allow the excitement and authority of the role to fill us with ideas about who we want our children to be: the personalities they'll have, the interests they'll develop, the hobbies they'll pick up. But we forget to take time to get to actually know our children. My job is not to decide who my kids are. My job is to get to know them, really get to know them, and then be their cheerleader and help them make the most of their strengths, even the ones I might find annoying at times. (And, trust me, there are things about your kids' personalities that will annoy you. Totally normal! There are things about your personality that annoy them, too.)

Think about it this way: we don't buy tickets for the best seats in the house to a brand-new, never-before-seen play and then walk into the theater having already decided exactly how each scene should look and who each character is. Where is the fun in that? We walk into the theater with our minds completely open. We pay attention to every line, every detail, every emotion, every scene change. We don't write the script as we watch the play; we let it all unfold before our eyes. We let it surprise us. And hopefully, we learn from it.

We spend a lot of time and effort teaching our kids to respect others, but I think it is also important that we show a certain amount of respect for our kids as human beings and relate to them as real people, not as prototypes of who kids (even *our* kids) "should" be.

To be clear, this doesn't mean I'm the "cool mom." I believe in discipline and rules. But I strive to spend as much time learning who my children are as I spend cultivating traits I hope will take root, like kindness and trustworthiness. They are motoring along their own paths of social, physical, and intellectual development, propelled by their own blend of strengths, weaknesses, and quirks. I may never get to know them if I tell them who they are before they've had a chance to figure it out for themselves.

When I was nineteen years old, I was babysitting a little five-year-old girl. She kept drawing picture after picture, and as I sat there watching her draw, I asked, "Do you want to be an artist when you grow up?"

"What do you mean?"

"An artist," I replied. "Is that what you want to be when you grow up?"

She looked at me, confused, and said, "But I already am an artist."

She was right. She didn't need to wait to grow up in order to be an artist. She already was one. Childhood is not a rehearsal for life; childhood is life and children are already whole people.

Part of the process of getting to know my children is helping them figure out what they're passionate about. And when I say passionate, I don't mean just, "What do you love?" I also want to know, "What angers you? What angers you about the world? What breaks your heart?" Pay attention to all of the strong emotions, whether they're good or bad, because intensity shows how genuinely they care about something. If I can get my kids to pinpoint what really makes them *feel* and then combine that with who they are—hyper, talkative, patient, great at math—I can help them begin to map out what they're meant to do with their lives. Careers evolve a lot over a lifetime, and if we attach our self-worth to our job titles, we set ourselves up for an identity crisis if our careers don't pan out. But if we focus on the bigger question, the deeper one, of where our passions and our gifts intersect, it becomes easy to pivot and work with whatever life throws at us while still maintaining our sense of self and purpose.

Being in the entertainment industry now, the "you're too much of this" or "you're not enough of that" never ends. Whether I'm hearing it from people with years of experience in my field or from fans, I still regularly receive suggestions about how I should change myself, everything from the way I look to the way I sound to my personality. I'm so thankful for that unsettled feeling I had during *The Ambush Cook,* because it's been a great reminder that faking it feels miserable and exhausting, and authenticity, though it sometimes feels vulnerable, is freeing and powerful.

No, I will not change who I am, no matter how big a title or paycheck you offer me. No, I will not portray my life as perfect. No, I will not stop being vulnerable. No, I will not "calm down." I will not be quiet. I will not stop being sassy or sarcastic. I will not move my hands less when I'm talking. I will not talk like "a normal person," whatever that means. I have stopped being who I think others need me to be, and now I am just who I am.

The characteristics that attracted the most criticism have turned out to be my most powerful tools, once I learned to use them wisely. The traits that I got in trouble for as a kid are the same traits that led to my success. Now I get paid to talk too much, to be too transparent, to be too hyper, to be too much. I was sure these quirks were what was holding me back, when in reality, what held me back was desperately trying to change those genuine parts of myself, instead of trying to figure out how to turn them into my superpowers.

What if being super curious and outgoing doesn't mean I'm desperate for attention? What if it means that life intrigues me and excites me and I want to share that excitement with others? What if being sensitive doesn't mean I'm weak? What if it just means I feel deeply, for myself and also for others? Don't we need more of that in this world? What if being talkative isn't a bad thing? What if it just means that I pay attention to every detail so I can tell a great story? What if all the traits we've been told are negative are actually our greatest strengths?

Parenting is about raising myself as much as it is about raising my kids. I try to nurture the small voice that's in the back of all our heads. It's the voice that says, "You are worthy of care. You are safe. You are loved. You are unique. And you still have a hell of a lot to learn, whether you're five or eighty-five." What kids need and what adults need aren't so different, and most of us need a daily reminder that who we are is enough. We all have a calling in life. It doesn't have to be something extravagant; it doesn't have to save the world. Your calling might not even necessarily be a part of your career, but we all have strengths and talents and passions, and when we turn up the volume on those, and turn down the volume on all the outside voices, that's when we find true success.

My calling is to be for others what I needed when I was a young, single mother who felt scared, lost, and inadequate. And the only way I can be successful at that is to be completely authentic. In the process, hopefully I will teach my kids to be authentic as well.

Oh, and in case I forgot to mention it, there was this one time when I was standing in a parking lot, eating hot dogs with Oprah. And she liked me just the way I was. Those were good times. But these are better. Because now I finally like myself, too. Just the way I am. Authenticity. It feels like a warm, soothing bath.

Three

Falling Apart

I needed to leave my marriage, and I didn't have a plan.

To everyone in my life this seemed like an impulsive decision after five years of marital bliss. It wasn't impulsive. And it wasn't marital bliss.

Not long after my first wedding anniversary, I found myself crammed into the tiny bathroom of the one-bedroom apartment just north of Boston that I was sharing with my husband while he was getting his master's degree, closely examining a friend's pee.

She and her husband had been trying to have a baby, but she was too nervous to take a pregnancy test. She was scared of how disappointed she would feel if the result was negative.

"So come over!" I told her. "Bring an extra test and we'll both do it. Maybe if you have someone else waiting for results with you, it will make it less stressful. We can have a pee party!"

I knew I wasn't pregnant.

My marriage had just started, but it was already falling apart. Things had gotten so chilly between my husband and me that we barely showed each other any affection let alone enough to make a baby.

So while I leaned against the sink and tried not to bump knees with my friend as she perched on the edge of the tub, I was all too pleased to focus my attention on her. And her pee. She was nervous and hopeful. I was nervous and hopeful for her.

"Now, listen. Even if it's negative," I assured her, "it could happen next month, so either way, everything is okay." We slowly approached the tests and both focused our eyes on hers. It was positive! And then I looked at mine.

Holy crap.

It was also positive.

While my friend jumped up and down and gushed about how fun it was going to be trading maternity outfits, I was trying to figure out the best way to gently suggest she go see her doctor for a real test. Because the over-the-counter two-pack she'd bought was clearly defective.

I *couldn't* be pregnant. My husband and I hadn't been trying to get pregnant. I was still on birth control, and we'd had sex only once in the past few months. Our family of two was fracturing. We were not trying to expand it.

Hours later, I was still sitting in my tiny bathroom, this time alone and on the floor. I couldn't take my eyes off the two little pink lines on my test. I dug the wrinkled instructions out of the garbage can and reread them, searching for proof that I had done it wrong. I peed the wrong way. I didn't use the right angle. I peed too much. Or not enough. Is Croatian urine different from

American urine? The test didn't say "international" on the box. Had I eaten something that day that screwed up the test results?

I dialed the customer service phone number on the side of the box and waited for my turn to speak with a representative. As I listened to the same saxophone solo for the fourth time, I flipped the box around in my hands, looking for the serial number so that the representative could confirm this test was part of a bad batch the company was probably already recalling. Finally, an agent with a wholesome midwestern accent picked up. "Hi, this is Shelley, how may I direct your call?"

"Hi . . . ummm . . . I just took a pregnancy test, and ummm . . . well . . . it says I'm pregnant. But I'm not pregnant. So I might have done it wrong, but more likely, I think the test is broken. And well . . . see . . . There are women out there who've been try-ing to get pregnant for years and can't, and if someone in that situation bought one of your broken tests and falsely thought she was pregnant, that would be devastating. So I'm just calling to let you know that some of your tests are broken. Because I'm sure you don't want to give people false hope, you know?"

The woman working for the obviously bogus, fake, broken pregnancy test company replied in the most saccharine, conde-scending tone, "Sweetheart, do you have a mom or a grandma around you could open up to about this? Everything will be okay, you just need to talk to someone who can support you through this."

She thought I was a teenager! I immediately disliked her, sourly imagining a woman with a really bad perm and a judg-mental look on her face who probably never had sex or, when she did, had it only in the missionary position. "I'm a grown-up," I replied, annoyed. "I'm a grown-up who is married and really, really wants children. Someday."

Someday. But not today. Not at a time in my life when I was contemplating divorce.

After a little more arguing with Shelley, I called Karen, a friend who is a delivery nurse, and explained the situation.

"I'm working today, so just come in. I'll give you a quick blood test and call you back with results within a couple of hours," she said.

Karen took my blood in the hallway of the hospital's delivery ward, where I could hear the miracle of life coming at us from all sides. Karen snapped off her gloves and told me she'd call me around 4:00 with the results. She was excited. You see, she had no idea my marriage was in trouble.

A few minutes before 4:00 p.m., I shut myself in the closet, phone in hand, and waited. My husband was back from his class and I wanted to be alone. It was December in Hamilton, Massachusetts, just north of Boston, not far from where I'd gone to high school, and I struggled to find a comfortable space between the sweaters and puffy coats. My heart was pounding, but I was still certain that I wasn't pregnant. This wasn't in the plan. The plan was to plan my pregnancies. The plan had also been to never contemplate divorce.

The phone rang. Karen somehow intuitively knew that I needed her to be gentle with me.

"Kristina, are you sitting down?"

"No. Why? Do I need to be sitting down?"

"Yes, I need you to sit down."

I crouched down on the closet floor, trying not to trip over my husband's shoes.

"Kristina, you're pregnant. Without a doubt."

Immediately the tears came. And so did the love.

Just a few hours earlier I'd felt almost tipsy with confusion about what was happening, but in that instant, the fog I'd been shuffling through fell away to reveal a crystal-clear vision of what would be my new world.

I'd always wanted to be a mother, for as long as I could remember. I knew I was meant to be a mother the way some people just need to play music; it's like water to them—they can't live without it. The timing was terrible, the circumstances not what I ever would have dreamed of or planned, but somehow, the second I knew I was actually going to be a mother, I felt myself wrapped in love and conviction. Every ounce of "this can't be happening" instantly left me and was replaced by such deep, overwhelming love for this child. I stayed in the closet for a little while, crying, whispering to my baby, "You are so loved. You are so wanted."

Then I walked into the living room where my husband was sitting in a blue leather recliner, a hand-me-down from my parents. I gently took the Kierkegaard book he was reading from him, closed it, put it down, and sat on his lap. This act alone was more affection than we had shown each other in weeks.

"I'm pregnant," I said. Just like that. The words came out of my mouth and made it even more real. This wasn't how I pictured telling my husband we were going to have a child. I always imagined I'd reveal the good news in some creative way with a scavenger hunt, a fortune cookie, a scrapbook, or some other romantic, movielike scene that would end in us crying and kissing and celebrating.

But complicated times beg for simplicity. My simple declaration was followed by a bare-bones conversation about the next steps. I don't remember all that was said, but I do remember confidently stating, "We will make this work." No way was my kid going to grow up in a broken home. After all, wanting kids was something we'd agreed on, back when we agreed on things.

Over the next few years, my husband and I went through the motions of being married. We had something in common now that was so important to both of us. Our baby boy had bonded us forever. Our love for each other didn't blossom, but the love we shared for him put us back on the same team. Whatever our differences and disagreements and incompatibilities, we were working together toward the same goal—to raise a healthy child—and that tunnel vision meant we could avoid looking too closely at our problems.

Ten months after the birth of our first child, Luka, I got pregnant with our daughter, Matea. This time there was no surprise, no dramatic phone call to a 1-800 customer service number, no crouching in a closet crying. We'd been trying. I wanted a bunch of kids. At least four. Preferably six. (But definitely not three! I was one of three children and I was usually the odd one out, so I knew that three was a bad number for kids.) I was determined to stay in my marriage, and I was determined to give Luka a sibling.

Matea's first year of life was a blur. Soon after she was born, my husband started a PhD program in Southern California and we moved across the country, far away from family and friends. Being a stay-at-home mom to two babies only a year and a half apart with no extended family or close friends around was, need-less to say, exhausting. But I loved being a mom. And I had ad-justed to pretending that my marriage was functioning well.

But there's only so long a person can go through the motions of pretending everything is okay when nothing is okay.

I'm not going to delve into all the reasons my marriage didn't work or why I finally decided to leave, because it wouldn't be fair to my children or my ex-husband, who I'm sure has his own ver-sion of events. And it wouldn't be fair to you, dear reader, to hear only one side of a complicated story that affects so many people.

Here is all you need to know: my marriage didn't fall apart suddenly. It came apart in pieces and stages, and we began to dis-mantle it soon after we started building it. The decision to divorce wasn't one I took lightly. Therapy sessions helped convince me there wasn't much hope, and I didn't file for divorce until I was ab-solutely sure that any possibility of my marriage ever healing was gone.

Leaving my marriage hurt. Leaving sucked. Leaving terrified me. Leaving was the scariest risk I've ever taken. Leaving made me feel like a failure. And yet not once did I look back and regret leaving.

No one goes into a marriage thinking it won't work. And when a marriage fails, it feels like a death. If there are kids in-volved, it feels like many deaths. Many slow, painful deaths. And when you're the one who is making the decision to pull the plug on a marriage, it can make you feel like the murderer.

Feeling confident in my decision to end the marriage didn't alleviate any of my guilt. And, as if my own guilt wasn't already too heavy for me to bear, there were people in my life who added to it, convinced that they were approaching my divorce with the best of intentions. People took sides, gave unsolicited advice, shamed me, tried to coax me into staying in a relationship they knew nothing about, analyzed and judged my grief, and believed they had the answers to how to fix all the pain. All of their work was aimed at preserving my marriage, but their efforts created more pain, more division, and more complications, with no positive results whatsoever.

I have to own my part in this. I kept my marital problems all to myself. I thought I was doing the right thing by pretending everything was okay. If I was determined to make the marriage work, what would be the point of blabbing to friends and family about the issues I was having with my husband? I didn't want to bad-mouth him. I didn't want to complain. I didn't want our marriage or either of us to be judged behind our backs. I didn't see the point of involving other people in our business when I was determined to stay.

I wish I had opened up just a little bit. I wish I had given some hints. I wish I had trusted the people in my life with my struggles along the way so that they wouldn't have felt so surprised when my marriage finally reached a breaking point. I genuinely thought I was doing the right thing by protecting the most fragile part of my life. But if I had it to do over, I would have reached out to my friends and family sooner.

Being blindsided by my situation brought out the worst in some of the people I was closest to and needed the most at the time. For some, simply saving my dysfunctional marriage became more important than hearing me out, more important than the truth, and much more important than compassion or love.

Part of me understood where they were coming from. I had wanted to stay in my marriage because I believed it was the best thing for my children. My husband was a good father, the kind who wanted to spend time with his kids and changed diapers and made meals and built Legos with Luka on the carpet for hours on end. But I also knew that our marriage was unhealthy. The older my kids got, the more I could see that I didn't want them to grow up with our relationship as their model for what marriage looks like.

Some people understood and listened and loved me, but I was so focused on those who were pushing back and judging me that I couldn't appreciate and embrace the people who were leaning in and accepting and helping me. A common human mistake. We say we hate negativity yet we fixate on it and let it distract us from all the good in our lives. And the judgment I felt from those who stood against me isolated me from those who would've stood beside me.

All the postdivorce drama felt so unnecessary, so loud and crippling, that I decided to tiptoe out of my marriage without adding any additional noise. I didn't want to fight for stuff or money, not that we even had much in the first place. I didn't want endless court battles. I just wanted to leave.

For the last few years of my marriage, I had stopped working outside the home and became a full-time stay-at-home mom—a job that, unfortunately, doesn't pay the six-figure salary it warrants. I slept on the couch of the apartment I still shared with my husband until I could find a job, find a place to live, and make everything official.

By this point, the tension between my soon-to-be ex and me

was unbearable. When I had first told him that I wanted to leave, he'd seemed to understand. We talked late into the night about why our marriage had fallen apart. We wept together, and we decided we would stay on friendly terms for the sake of our kids.

But all of the refereeing and the opinions of outside influences tainted our good intentions, and the tension in the apartment we still shared became suffocating.

After one particularly tense day, I decided to do an internet search for the most expensive restaurants in my town. (Expensive restaurant = larger bills = larger tips.) I wrote down the address of the very first restaurant that popped up on my screen and quickly typed up and printed a résumé. I had experience waiting tables, so this seemed like the most realistic job for me to get quickly and the best way for me to earn some cash fast.

I got dressed up. Nice pants, dressy shirt, dry shampoo in my hair, and a fake smile plastered on my face. I drove to the restaurant and walked in through the heavy double doors. Large fresh flower arrangements decorated the front lobby. A young hostess greeted me. She seemed so carefree, so light and cheerful, so far beyond my emotional state, that I wondered if we could really be breathing the same air, as if her atmosphere contained a high percentage of helium and tuberose while mine was composed primarily of swamp gas.

"Welcome! Meeting someone for lunch today, ma'am?"

I tried to match her airy tone, so as not to blow my cover. I knew no one would hire me if they knew what a shambles my life was.

"No, I'm not here for lunch. Actually . . . I'm here to get hired!

I need a job." I handed her my résumé. "I do have a lot of experience waiting tables."

She smiled sweetly. "Oh, I'm sorry. I don't think we're hiring,
but I will pass this along to the manager."

My face relaxed out of the smile I had been forcing and a tinge
of desperation entered my voice.

"Could I please talk to the manager? It won't take long."

"He's not available right now, but I will make sure he gets
your résumé."

I stared at her for a few seconds, not sure what to do. I didn't
want to leave. I didn't feel like I belonged anywhere. I just wanted
to stay there at that restaurant until someone gave me some
hope, gave me a job, so that I could finally move out of an apartment that was no longer mine.

"Okay. Great. I'll be back tomorrow."

The next day, I drove back to the restaurant and had nearly
the exact same conversation with a different person who was
working the front desk. The conversation ended with another
"Great. I'll be back tomorrow."

I was so desperate, yet I was too overwhelmed to come up
with a better plan—like perhaps applying to a dozen different
restaurants. My survival instinct had kicked in and so had my
feistiness and stubbornness, but my mind was too fogged by pain
to use those assets to form a multifaceted attack for launching
into my new life as a single, self-sufficient mom. All I knew was
that I had no money, no support system, and two young children
I needed to take care of. Day after day I returned to the same
restaurant, ending each visit with "Great. I'll be back tomorrow."

On day six, one of the managers approached me in the middle of my dialogue with the hostess, which at this point felt like déjà vu. As I saw him walking over to me, I knew I had a 10 percent chance of a job interview and a 90 percent chance of a restraining order.

The manager chuckled at me and said, "Okay, okay, you've worn me down. I'll give you an interview." He led me to the back corner of the fancy restaurant, where he asked me endless questions about wines I had never heard of.

Now, let me remind you that at this point in my life, I was feeling totally alone and desperate and scared and sad and confused. If I'd had my first choice, I wouldn't have been on the job hunt. I would have been in my pajamas in a dark room, avoiding social interactions. So the fact that I got fully dressed six days in a row, covered the dark bags under my eyes with thirteen thick layers of concealer, did my best not to look like I hated life (when I truly hated life), and drove to this place six different times, determined to get a job—and finally got an interview—was a huge achievement. There was no way I was going to let a little pop quiz about fermented grape juice stop me.

As the manager brought up different wines on the wine list, I made up descriptions and talked about the boldness of this wine and the oakiness of that one, hoping that if I spoke with enough confidence, I would sound legitimate.

Which is how I learned that even managers of fancy fine-dining establishments don't really know whether a glass of wine has notes of chocolate and cardamom or a buttery mouthfeel with hints of vanilla, almond, and pear. I basically just described a bunch of my favorite dessert recipes in wine terms and prayed he'd never tasted a marzipan tart.

My gamble paid off. And the next time I walked into that restaurant, I walked in as an employee.

Two months after I started my waitressing job, I found a small two-bedroom apartment and put down the money for the first month's rent and a security deposit. But I knew I wasn't going to be able to fully cover rent on my own, so my kids and I were going to need to have a roommate.

I scrambled to quickly find a perfect someone willing to move into a situation that would afford them a teensy private bedroom and common spaces they shared with three other people, two of whom threw the occasional tantrum. To make the living arrangement even more desirable, Luka—like many three-year-olds—often wet the bed, and the accident would always soak through his Pull-Up and into the mattress. This created a fun late-night ritual where I would drag his mattress into the living room, pour white vinegar on it, hit it with a hair dryer, pour baking soda over that, rub it in, vacuum up the baking soda, then drag the mattress back to our room, muscle it onto the top bunk again, then scoop up my son and deposit him back on the bed. (If I could have afforded it, I definitely would have added vodka to the routine.) So not only would my lucky cohabitant be woken by the dulcet tones of two toddlers jumping up and down clamoring for breakfast at 6:00 a.m., she could also enjoy the soothing serenade of a hair dryer and vacuum every night around 3:00 a.m. Who wouldn't love that?

After trying out a few different people, I finally, by some small miracle, found Karen, a kind, independent, straight-shooting woman who never planned on living with small children but somehow didn't want to kill mine. To this day, I have no idea why she agreed to cohabitate with a depressed, broke single mom and her two hyper toddlers. But I am eternally grateful to her for putting up with us.

The weeks that followed our move were packed with many hours of appointments and paperwork and waiting in long lines, one kid in a stroller and one in my arms, applying for food stamps, applying for Medi-Cal (a program in California that offers free or low-cost health coverage for children and adults with limited income and resources), trying to get Luka into a subsidized preschool for just a few hours a day, and, most important, trying desperately to make sure I didn't take all my stress and exhaustion and sadness out on my children. My children hadn't asked for any of this.

In order to receive government assistance for a whole slew of things, I had to prove that I had a job. Which meant that I had to walk into the upscale restaurant where I worked and ask my upscale boss in his upscale suit who lived in an upscale house to sign a form that basically said, as far as I was concerned at the time, I was a loser who couldn't feed her own kids. I was so embarrassed. I shouldn't have been because there is absolutely nothing wrong with getting help when you need it, but I was mortified.

During my first few months at the restaurant, no one knew my full story. I was such an emotional wreck that I worried if I opened up even just a little bit about my personal life, it would all come flooding out and I wouldn't have the strength to stop it. At work, I knew I had to hold it together and be professional. I couldn't risk losing my job.

I lied a lot during that time. I pretended a lot. I hid a lot of what I was really thinking and feeling. I just wanted to feel normal. I said and did anything and everything to make myself feel like a normal mom, a normal person, even though inside nothing felt normal and everything felt crazy.

In some ways, I was repeating the coping pattern I'd deployed in my marriage—pretending to those closest to me that everything was fine and not allowing anyone into my full, messy truth. So often when we are at our lowest, we close off, fists clenched. We isolate ourselves. And yet when we're at our lowest we should be opening up, leaning in, reaching out. I hated feeling alone, yet I wasn't letting anyone in. I was lucky that even as I pushed the world away, there were people who showed up for me. People who loved me when I couldn't love myself.

"I'm flying out to see you! I want to be there for you," my friend Jo, who lives across the country, insisted. She was a busy mom with three young kids, one who was an infant at the time. She didn't have space for my drama. But she loved me enough not to see me as an inconvenience.

"Why don't you let me watch the kids for the evening so that you can pick up an extra shift at work," my friend Melissa offered. And I learned to accept her help.

"I'm stopping by after work with some books for the kids," my friend Jonathan said. He was like a brother to me, like an uncle to my children. He was the one who bought my children bunk beds and once let me borrow eight hundred dollars to cover my rent. I will never forget how good I felt when I saved up enough to pay him back. I never wanted any of these wonderful people to feel I was taking advantage of them.

"I talked to my manager about the expired food we toss," my friend Dave, who worked at Starbucks, told me, "and said I knew a single mom who would really appreciate the food. It might be a little stale, but it's still good." So many mornings, my children and I ate semistale Starbucks muffins for breakfast. And I was so grateful.

My people showed up for me. I learned through my friendships with Jo and Melissa and Jonathan and Dave and so many others who loved me despite my crappy existence that I didn't have to walk through my hell alone. These wonderful people rallied around me and showed me that I deserved love and care, even when I felt worthless. With their help, I slowly came to understand that the reason I needed help from others wasn't because I was an inadequate human. I needed help simply because I was human.

We are not meant to go through this life alone. Name any situation you want to improve and I guarantee you, you'll get there faster and more effectively if you reach out to others. We want to be our best. But the truth is, our best is beyond us. We need others in order to be our best.

Years after my divorce, my friend Jonathan was visiting me from New Zealand, where he had moved for a job. We sat in my backyard eating lava cakes and reminiscing about the crazy years following my divorce. I blocked out so much of that time that my memories are blurry at best. So, out of genuine curiosity, I asked him, "What do you remember the most about me during that time?" I expected him to tell me how pathetic my life was, how he pitied me.

"The thing I remember the most, Kristina, is how much you hated yourself," he replied. "You gave yourself no credit for how strong you actually were, for the tireless efforts you took on daily to coordinate life and get your kids everything they needed. Instead, you just hated yourself."

His answer hit me hard. He was right. I hated myself. My friends hadn't seen me as someone deserving of hatred and pity, though. Only I did. And if they hadn't found me and been willing to show me love, I'd probably still feel that way. But I unclenched my fist and clutched, instead, the hands they extended to me. I slowly stopped hating myself and my life. It took letting people into my mess and seeing it through their eyes for me to find the goodness in me, in my situation.

And as for those who added to my pain after the divorce? Over the years, I have been able to reconcile with most of them, too. This is important to include. It's the story I needed to hear when I believed I'd be shunned and judged forever, that some of the people I loved the most would never be a part of my life again. I need you to know that if you're in pain, there is still hope. I need you to know that it is worth staying open. Most of all, I need you to know that the negativity thrown our way isn't always personal and people can change. Really change. So it's worth giving those who have written us off a chance to come around. And in our lowest moments, we need to welcome our people into our messy, imperfect lives. Give them a chance to hold us up. And give ourselves a chance, too—a chance to be loved even when we hate ourselves.

Four

Wednesday Night Dinners

In my darkest moments, I thought about taking my life. I never actually tried. I just thought about it. I wrote lists of pros and cons. I contemplated what would be the easiest way to go— physically for me and emotionally for everyone around me.

I know it's hard for people who have never been in such a dark place to understand how any mother could think about taking her own life. But parents who contemplate suicide don't feel that they are being selfish by leaving their children without a mom or a dad. Parents who contemplate suicide genuinely believe that their children will actually be better off without them, that their children's world will be easier and happier without their parent in it. You have to be in a hell of a lot of pain to think that way. I was in a hell of a lot of pain.

To say I was just sad would be an understatement.

I was depressed. Depressed as in "my doctor suggested all kinds of pills" depressed. Depressed as in "my friends were more than worried about me" depressed. Depressed as in "I gained twenty pounds in one month" depressed. You know you're a mess when your doctor is handing you a brochure on antidepressants and a brochure on Weight Watchers all in the same visit. You start asking yourself, "How did I get here?" You start telling yourself, "There's no way out of here."

And I was still struggling financially. Another understatement. I was broke. Broke as in "sleeping on the floor in a small bedroom I shared with my two children" broke. Broke as in "looking up homeless shelters in the area in case I couldn't afford to keep paying rent" broke. Broke as in "I'd started stealing toilet paper and tampons from the restaurant where I worked because I couldn't afford basic hygiene products" broke. (Years later, I finally confessed to one of the managers. They forgave me.)

At night I would lie awake next to the bunk beds my friend had generously bought for my kids because I didn't have the money to do so myself. It wasn't the physical discomfort of sleeping on the floor that kept me up; it was mental torment. My routine of nighttime anxiety that started the moment Luka was born was intensifying:

Are my kids getting enough nutritious food? Are my kids getting enough exercise? Do my kids have enough toys? Do I have the right toys? Are we playing enough educational games? When my son was telling me that story, did he know I was ignoring him because I was doing something else or did he feel heard and seen? Is the free preschool he's attending good enough? Was his tantrum because he was tired or was it because of something that happened at school? Do I know

everything about my kids' lives? Am I paying enough atten-
tion? Does it matter that my child saw me naked today? At
what point should children not see their parents naked? I lost
my patience and I snapped at my kid today—how will those
negative words shape him? Am I supposed to give them more
than just a daily vitamin? What's the right ratio of vegetables
to carbs? Does it matter that the milk I got for free from that
WIC program isn't organic? Is my daughter going to grow
boobs at age five because she's not getting organic milk? Are
we all going to get cancer from the pesticides?

My run-of-the-mill maternal concerns had mushroomed in my mind until living with them didn't feel manageable. The water was getting too high and I didn't have the stamina to keep paddling.

Because I hid the jagged edges of my marriage until I announced my intention to get a divorce, some had perceived me to be a selfish, terrible mother bent on ruining her family. It was unspeakably painful to have people I loved so much think so little of me. After a while, I couldn't help but wonder, *Am I really a horrible person?* I started to become convinced that my children, the two most important people in my life, deserved so much more than the crappy, depressed, selfish, home-wrecking, broke loser mother they'd been saddled with, one who had to apply for food stamps because she couldn't even meet their most basic needs.

At night, I began to wonder if I really mattered, if my life mattered, if any of it was worth struggling for.

I was also lonely. Another understatement. Even though I was lucky to have a cadre of friends who continually stood by me, I still felt really, really lonely. You don't have to be completely alone in order to feel deeply alone. And I was bitter, and angry, and confused, and cynical, and miserable, and, yes, those are all understatements, too.

When you get like that, when you fall so deeply into your misery, you become self-consumed—or at least I did. I lived and breathed and ate and drank and made out with self-pity. I didn't *talk* about it constantly. I didn't share my sob story with everyone I met. I mostly just kept it in and wallowed in it behind closed doors.

Do you know what someone who is deeply struggling looks like? Most often, she looks just like you. She looks like someone who might not be deeply struggling. My theater degree came in handy, as I showed up to each work shift convincingly playing the part of a confident, put-together, recently divorced mother of two who is doing just fine. I made jokes, joined in on pranks the staff would play on one another, and lied a lot when asked by customers or coworkers about my personal life or my state of mind.

At the end of almost every shift, around midnight, I'd order the restaurant's signature flatbread. Employees got 50 percent off, so this was a cheap dinner for me. I'd get in my car, place the cardboard pizza box in my lap, and start to cry. Understatement. I'd sob. All the way home, I'd sob while stuffing my face with the yummy crust, covered in greasy caramelized pears, roasted walnuts, and stinky, creamy, delicious Cambozola cheese. All the emotions I had held in for hours while on my shift would pour out during my drive back to reality, where I'd no longer get to pretend my life was easy or good. The flatbread became my grieving buddy, my comfort food. By the time I would pull up to my apartment complex, there were only a few bites left, always soaked in my tears. (Not trying to sound poetic here. They were literally soaked in my tears.)

I'd park my car and just sit there. Sometimes for hours. I mostly worked weekends while my kids were with their dad, and I hated being alone in the room I shared with them. That room was just another reminder of how little I had, and when my children weren't around, I felt like I had nothing. They were all that mattered. Everything else sucked. I'd sit in my car, radio off, in complete silence, while every bad thing anyone had ever said about me played on a loop in the background like the worst movie soundtrack ever. I knew I was a failure by every metric there was.

On one of those nights in my car, alone with my thoughts, I decided I'd had enough of myself. I was disgusted by how low I had sunk, but instead of contemplating ending it all, I gave my feisty side permission to kick in.

My mother will tell you that my feistiness was there from the moment I came out of her screaming. I was born with it in spades, but I also think feistiness is something that can be learned. Like all personality traits, being a stubborn, scrappy fighter has advantages and disadvantages, but it's an important tool to keep in your toolbox. Because while feistiness can lead you to make crazy decisions that would have benefited from just a *little* more forethought, it can also get you off your butt and ready to fight for your life.

That night, my feisty inner voice rose up against the negative ones with rebellious fire. My feistiness told me that I was the one contributing to my own misery by being passive about it and allowing it to consume every fiber of my being. It told me that I had more power than I realized and I could part ways with my unhappy state. That inner voice was passionate, and that passion was able to temporarily overpower the apathy that had consumed me so that I could make an important realization: the only way I'd ever get out of this "poor me" state was to stop focusing on myself and start looking outside my pathetic little life. And the best way to do that, I thought, would be to volunteer somewhere.

If I could somehow help others in need, it would distract me from my own neediness. Now, there was the first brilliant thought I had had in a while! It might be the most brilliant thought I had *ever* had. (Not an understatement.)

The next morning, I picked up the phone and started calling various organizations, asking if I could become a volunteer. At that time Matea was two and Luka was barely four. I couldn't afford a babysitter, and while my kids were with their dad on the weekends, I was always working. During the day on weekends, I had picked up an additional part-time job bookkeeping for a different restaurant, so I was busy pretending I was brainy enough to be trusted with grown-up things like spreadsheets and budgets. I could volunteer only during the week, when my kids were with me. Naturally, I assumed they would volunteer alongside me. But no homeless shelter, hospital, soup kitchen, or any other sane organization I called wanted hyper, little two- and four-year-olds "volunteering."

After being told the same thing over and over again—"We'd love to have you, but your kids are too young"—I gave up. I was already feeling like a loser, so getting rejected from volunteering, regardless of the reason, upgraded me to a whole new level of losership! (It's a word.) Finally, I'd had my first brilliant thought— my first constructive idea for how to save myself from my stupid self-pity and misery—and even that had failed.

That same old record started spinning in my head: *I am a complete failure. Every idea and thought I have is useless. I am useless. I have nothing to offer. I don't know how to do anything.* Okay, not completely true. I'm pretty decent at changing diapers and I do know how to cook a great meal with next to nothing, but that's it. That's all I know how to do. And considering how many times my boy has pissed on me during a diaper change, even my diaper-changing skills could use some improvement. So there you have it. The only thing I'm good at is cooking. So what? Who cares if I can make my kids a great dinner? They're too young to really appreciate it, and it's definitely not changing the world, and I'm definitely still a total worthless loser.

Suddenly my mind lit up with memories of the years I spent cooking with my grandmother, cooking for friends' birthday parties and baby showers, cooking for my sister's wedding reception. No matter where I was in life, no matter how I felt about myself, through all the ups and downs, the one thing I'd always felt confident about was feeding people. If I couldn't find a place that would let me volunteer, why not *create* a place to volunteer? Just because no soup kitchen in a thirty-mile radius would let me serve their soup didn't mean I couldn't feed people. I could feed people *in my home*.

I was learning an important lesson that would come in handy for the rest of my life: Don't accept no as an answer. See it as a challenge, as a question. "No? Not this way? No problem. I'll find another way."

That evening, I impulsively (something I'm really good at), without really thinking it through (also really good at that), wrote an email and sent it to everyone I knew in the LA area.

Subject: Wednesday Night Dinners

Dear friends,

Starting this coming Wednesday, I will be cooking for anyone who needs a meal. Please think of people you know who are either struggling financially and could use a free dinner, or perhaps a college kid who is sick of cafeteria food, or someone new to town who is lonely and needs to make some friends, or maybe an elderly person who just lost their spouse and is feeling lonely, or anyone else who would appreciate homemade food and good company. Invite them to my place. I will feed everyone. My door will be wide open starting at 6:00 p.m.

Love you all,
Kristina

I didn't have a plan. But unlike all the other chaos in my life that I couldn't control, this was a crisis of my own making, one that felt manageable, and I was hoping the adrenaline and excitement that fueled this new idea would kick-start my creativity and give me some momentum.

I woke up early that Wednesday and went to a place I had become very familiar with: the 99 Cent Store. The 99 Cent Store and I were pretty much dating at that point and I was fully committed. When you're poor, dollar stores make you feel like you're doing all right. You walk out of there carrying not one but two or three bags of stuff that you actually paid for yourself without using food stamps, and you start feeling like you just went on a fancy shopping spree. I loved that store, I trusted it, and it always came through for me. Total confidence booster.

That Wednesday, I purchased a bunch of bags of pasta and then I found some fresh vegetables and even some cheese. I wasn't aiming for a gourmet meal or following a specific recipe. I was just trying to create the most delicious-tasting dinner I could on a tight budget for a lot of people. Or no people.

Would anyone show up? Would my friends even take my email seriously, since they knew what a pathetic mess I was? My stubbornness won out against my negativity and I cleaned the little apartment I shared with my roommate, cooked the biggest pot of pasta I'd ever cooked, and baked some homemade rolls (much cheaper than buying them).

Luka has been a chatty, maître d' type since he learned to talk, so I put him in charge of offering our guests water (aka the one beverage I wouldn't mind him spilling—and the only one I could afford anyway). Matea was a well-mannered, semianti-social child at the time, so I gave her the very important job of handing out napkins. It was the perfect task to make her feel helpful yet allow her to run away from the guests without having to schmooze.

Then 5:30 p.m. rolled around, and I got nervous. Really nervous. I started chewing on the skin around my fingernails and pacing. *What if no one shows up? What if my friends are embarrassed to bring people to my little apartment? What if they're embarrassed to introduce people to someone like me? What if I just spent this whole day cooking and cleaning for nothing? What if my idea is stupid? What if the one and only thing I feel I have to offer fails? What if? What if? What if?* (Those two words are each quite lovely on their own, but when you pair them up . . . what a downer.)

At 6:00 sharp, with bleeding nailbeds, I opened the front door. No one was there. There was a lot of pasta in my kitchen—*a lot* of pasta, and no one at my front door. I felt like I was being stood up. Not by a boy. But by hope.

But within five or ten minutes, three or four people showed up. Then more people came. And then even more. By the end of the evening, I had made a second batch of pasta, run out of napkins, met a lot of new faces, and fed approximately thirty people. *Thirty* people! In my tiny little apartment. On my tiny little budget. With my tiny little kids who, by the way, proved to be incredible at pouring water and handing out napkins.

I will never forget shutting the door after my last guest left. I sat on the floor and cried. Understatement. I sobbed like a baby. But this wasn't the same sobbing with despair I had done night after night sitting alone in my car. This was different. That Wednesday night I sobbed like a broken little girl who had just experienced her first glimmer of healing. There was something so powerful, so magical and wonderful—and above all, peaceful—about the fact that I could feed all those people. I had been convinced that I had nothing to give, yet when I gave the little that I had, the results were something so much bigger than I ever could have expected.

The following day I started hearing from people who had come to my Wednesday Night Dinner. These people were so thankful, so happy. They told me how much they enjoyed my cooking, how nice it was to eat a homemade meal. Some told me they had just moved to town a few weeks before and that the dinner made them feel less homesick.

And that right there was a turning point for me. I don't remember ever feeling completely hopeless after that. Sure, I felt sad at times, angry and scared, but I didn't feel defeated or desperate. Because for the first time in a long time, I didn't feel useless. Even when I thought I had nothing, I still had something to offer. I, Kristina, have something to offer. I, Kristina, am worth something. Understatement.

It would have been easy to take that incredible feeling I had after the first Wednesday Night Dinner and assume all would now go well for me. But I knew that a turning point doesn't equal a onetime fix. As I continued with Wednesday Night Dinners, friends would often drop off ingredients to make sure I could afford to continue hosting those evenings. People started bringing salads and sides to round out the single giant pot of rice or pasta or potatoes I was serving that night, and executives in three-piece suits rubbed elbows with college students and other people struggling even more than I'd felt I was. There were so many interesting, open hearts walking through my door, and I was feeding them.

The people closest to me knew that these dinners were much more about me helping myself than me helping others. I needed those days of cooking for strangers more than those strangers needed my cooking. I needed the weekly reminder that I don't need to have a lot to give a lot, and that it takes only a small helping to feed the soul. In this case, my soul.

We humans crave a quick fix to our problems. But going from

hating your life to tolerating your life to feeling like your life is good or maybe even amazing doesn't happen overnight. It happens slowly. Because life is cruel that way. Or maybe because our patience needs to be tested at every turn. Or maybe, just maybe, because the things we get quickly and easily carry less significance. And not as many lessons. And without lessons, just as quickly as we make some progress, we're right back to where we started. Clueless and lost.

I remember in my hardest days being told that there is light at the end of the tunnel. That's super cute on a fridge magnet or a key chain, but when I was deep in my misery, a beautiful quote like that from a well-intentioned friend, which under normal circumstances would have encouraged me and given me hope, sounded dismal and empty. It was cheesy gibberish that didn't apply to someone like me. Misery can be deafening. It's like wearing earmuffs. Misery earmuffs. You're listening hard for encouragement, but it all sounds like nonsense that definitely wouldn't work for you.

Escaping from complete misery is not like driving through a straight, dark tunnel toward the light waiting to embrace you at the end. It feels more like crawling neck-deep in muck through the darkest, scariest, muddiest bat-filled cave of your nightmares with so many twists and turns that the light is rarely visible at all. And then continually choosing to search for the light, believing against all evidence that it exists and is reachable.

That kind of crawling is exhausting. It takes time. It takes feistiness. And if you can leaven that feistiness with a whole lot of patience, you'll save yourself an enormous amount of frustration. Because I'm not terribly patient, I was frequently frustrated. What

I learned through my slow crawl out of that cave was that I already had the tools I needed to get unstuck. I just hadn't been using them.

It's easy to overthink things, to judge your ideas and make excuses for why you should wait for this or that to happen before you take a proactive role in dragging yourself out of your misery. When you're sitting passively, hoping something will change but not actually doing anything to catalyze change, you start to get numb. It's like sitting on the floor in the same position for hours and hours and then trying to stand up. Your muscles are tight. Standing up is uncomfortable. And the last thing you want when you're already miserable is more discomfort, especially when you're not guaranteed, in writing, signed and notarized, that moving on will change anything. But going from "everything sucks" to "life is good" requires discomfort. And blind faith. It's not easy. It's not quick. It's mostly moving forward, but occasionally tripping and falling backward and getting bruises on top of bruises and having to pick yourself up and keep pushing forward again. The outcome we crave is often found by taking the steps we keep trying to resist.

I'm sure I could have easily spent months (or forever) planning out every detail of how I would throw my first Wednesday Night Dinner, writing lists and questioning myself at every turn. But I had to just get up and actually do it. When you're feeling helpless or hopeless, stop thinking about how helpless and hopeless you feel and just do something. Do something positive. Do something that matters. Do something without focusing on the list of things that could get in the way. Do not let the few things that are completely out of your control, control you completely.

After the war started in my home country of Croatia, an incredible man named Zorislav Laksar, who had no formal training in art, felt the need to create something out of all the destruction the war was causing. He would walk around after brutal, deadly attacks, looking for shrapnel from the grenades that were thrown on our city. He would pick up the shrapnel, take it home, and use it to build amazing sculptures. My parents had one of his sculptures, and on my fortieth birthday, they gave it to me, knowing how meaningful it is to me. The sculpture depicts a mother walking with her child. The child is holding the mother's hand and holding on to her teddy bear. It's a stunning work of art created completely from shrapnel, from something that had literally destroyed homes and killed people.

Wednesday Night Dinners were my sculptures. I had no formal training in cooking, but I knew that I had to stop passively staring at all the destroyed pieces of my life and instead build something meaningful out of them.

I still occasionally visit the restaurant where I waited tables during those dark days. Every time I return to have dinner there, I order my old grieving buddy, that delicious flatbread. I ask for it to go. I get in my car, open the cardboard box, and eat it while driving home. I don't sob. I don't feel alone. I don't feel hopeless. Because life no longer sucks. But I like the reminder. I like to remember what I've gone through so that I don't take anything for granted. I like to remember how I crawled out so that I never feel completely helpless again. It's the reason I still carry my old food stamps card in my wallet. It hasn't been active for years. But I still keep it right behind my credit card, so that every time I pull that credit card out to pay for something, I'm reminded of where I was and how far I've come.

One day during that first year after my divorce, I pulled out the food stamps card to pay for my groceries with one kid in my arms and the other sitting in the grocery cart. The woman behind me, sort of under her breath but loud enough to make sure I heard her, said, "Why don't you get a job instead of mooching off the government?" It felt like a punch in the face. My eyes welled up with tears and my hands started shaking. Though I was working two jobs at the time, I couldn't stand up for myself in that moment. I said nothing. Because I felt worthless as a person. I maybe even felt like I deserved that punch. Holding on to my food stamps card is a reminder that if I'm ever back in that place, I am not stuck. There is a way out, and I have all the tools I need to rise up. I just have to choose to utilize them.

When we're in the midst of despair, it feels so permanent, doesn't it? But a bad year or two or five doesn't equal a bad life. It equals a bad year or two or five. And getting to a better place is as simple as it is difficult: Keep moving forward. Stop worrying about what you're not, and start focusing on what you are. Stop worrying about what you don't have, and start focusing on what you do have. Dwelling on the negative will leave you stuck, and you can't get to a better place if you're standing still. So on those days when you don't have the strength to walk another baby step, crawl. Even if it's uncomfortable. The only way out is through. No detours. No waiting. Just keep moving forward. And you will get there. Stronger and better than ever. Understatement.

Five

The G Spot: Guilt, Grades, and Grace

When my son Luka was nine, he was completely obsessed with the *Titanic*. He hadn't seen the movie, a romantic tragedy, which was loosely based on the 1912 sinking of the luxury ship, because I didn't think it was age appropriate, but he did have books on the *Titanic* and knew things about the ship and its first (and last) voyage that I had never known. Like the fact that there were only two bathtubs available for more than seven hundred third-class passengers. Or that Milton Hershey, the founder of Hershey's chocolate, purchased tickets to be aboard the *Titanic* but canceled his reservation at the last minute (a big relief for my chocoholic son). So for Luka's ninth birthday, I decided to make him a *Titanic* cake.

Elaborate cakes have become a birthday tradition in our family. I've made everything from various animal-shaped cakes to a chessboard with edible, movable chess pieces to a toilet cake with poop-shaped brownie bites in it.

If you're looking for a tutorial on how to make your kid a fabulous cake, here it is: bake a normal cake. Then stay up all night cutting, assembling, and rearranging cake pieces like a puzzle while googling hundreds of photos of the shape you're trying to re-create. Use fourteen thousand pounds of butter to make enough frosting to cover up all your mistakes. By the time you're completely exhausted, delirious, covered in flour, butter, and sugar, sweating in desperation, and asking yourself, *Why do I do this to myself?!? I should have just bought a cake like normal people do!* the cake will almost be finished but will still look like crap. Then, after a few more hours of torture and regret, voilà . . . the cake will be complete.

Midmorning on the day of my son's ninth birthday party, I was in my kitchen feeling exhausted and stressed-out. I was covered in so much gray frosting that if you'd seen me out of context, you might have assumed I was suffering from some obscure but severe form of dermatitis. I was rushing to cut up some fruit before all his friends arrived when the knife slipped. I gashed myself and screamed at the top of my lungs, "Shit!"

At that time, Luka had never heard me say a bad word. In this one area, I had been a generally successful mom, watching my mouth around my kids. Except for the word "crap." That one doesn't count. It's not a bad word. It's just the reality of my life. Literally and metaphorically, my life is full of crap. Other than that, I had been really good about my language around my children. But there I was, half an hour before my son's birthday party, with him standing right next to me, screaming, "Shit!"

His face turned white. He stared at me. "Mom? Mom, you . . . you just said a really bad . . . I can't believe you said . . . I . . ." He couldn't even get the sentence out. He was so shocked and disappointed that his mother could have said that word. And so loudly! (I know, I know, he was a sheltered little kid. Sheltered and utterly oblivious to one of his mother's greatest gifts: vulgarity.)

Instead of just admitting it, apologizing, and using the moment as an opportunity for a lesson, like a mature grown-up would, I said, "What do you mean? I . . . I didn't say a bad word." I avoided eye contact because, unlike cursing, lying well is not one of my talents. And then, panicked, I continued, "What's your cake? What's that cake that you wanted me to make?"

"The *Titanic.*"

"Right! And what is the *Titanic?*"

"What do you mean? Uh, it's a boat, Mom."

"No . . . it's a ship. It's a *ship.* Right? And that's what I screamed. Ship!!! Because I was reminding myself to take the *ship* cake out of the fridge so that your friends would see it. I didn't want your party to be ruined if I forgot to serve the cake. The ship cake. Ship!"

Deep down inside, I was hoping that my son would call me out on my lie, but instead, he looked at me with such sad eyes. "Mom, I'm so sorry. I'm so sorry that I accused you of saying something bad, and you didn't even do that. You were just caring about me and wanted to make sure that my friends would see my cool cake. I'm so sorry."

If I were a good human being, I would have backpedaled immediately and said, "You know what? I lied. Mommy lied. Don't feel bad. Mommy did say a bad word. You don't have to feel bad about anything." But I didn't. Which is why I will probably burn in hell. Years later, I still feel guilty about that conversation, which is only like the 3,586th thing on the rotating platter of regret that I lie awake picking over every single night. So I'd like to dedicate this chapter to dealing with guilt, the powerful force that has ruined pretty much every night of sleep for me over the past sixteen years.

Guilt is a funny thing. There are times we should feel some guilt because we've done something wrong. Without the cue that guilty feeling transmits, we're bound to just keep repeating the same offense. But then there are times when we feel guilty about things that don't merit our attention, things that aren't necessarily wrongdoings but just normal human doings that we perceive to be negative and that we fixate on until they poison us.

I think guilt is a little like mascara. There is an appropriate, recommended amount to use—just enough to highlight those lashes to bring out their full potential. But if you apply fifty thousand layers of mascara, your lashes are going to look clumpy and gross, and you'll probably end up with a freaking eye infection. Guilt works the same way, and piling it on is not a good look. The guilt complex is one of the things nobody warns you about when you get pregnant or decide to adopt. Your friends and family will warn you about numerous challenges you're going to have to deal with, but nobody warns you about the abuse you're going to experience—not from your children, not from your spouse, but from yourself. No one mentions all the guilt mascara you will inevitably pile on until it looks like two baby tarantulas have crawled onto your face.

The "shit" conversation with my son might be worth feeling guilty about because there are actual lessons for me to learn there. Maybe that's one layer of guilt mascara. But why am I always piling on all these other unnecessary layers? I'm talking about layers of guilt like the fact that by the end of each day, I have rarely accomplished everything on my to-do list. Human. The projects I meant to be done with months ago, I haven't even started. Human. The people who are waiting to hear back from me on something are beginning to get annoyed. Human. The fact that I accidentally double-booked something on my schedule. Human. The text messages I haven't replied to yet. Human. The lame excuse I made for not wanting to play another never-ending round of Monopoly with my kid. Definitely human. And definitely not worthy of another layer of mascara.

Part of the issue is that we lump all our failures into the same category, in the "you suck and you should stay up all night feeling like crap about this" category. But the thing is, there's more than one category. Forgetting to set my alarm and getting my kids to school an hour late? That's an accidental failure. It doesn't belong in the deep, tormenting guilt category. The one time (today) that I completely lost my patience? That's a semiaccidental "I'm trying, but I'm an exhausted human" type of failure. Also completely not worth losing sleep over. Betraying someone or being mean or dismissive? Those are more deliberate, self-centered failures that show me where I need to work on myself. And then there's a whole other category of failures that feel very personal but actually have very little or maybe absolutely nothing to do with me (like all the times I failed to get a job I really wanted). I used to be an expert at dwelling on even the smallest failure for days, as if the outcomes of all my ventures should be completely in my control, as if everything I do belongs in the deliberate, self-centered failures category when really most of what I fail at on a day-to-day basis belongs in the "let it go" category.

Guilt can be a lot like that obnoxious guy who's been hitting on you for years and you continue to hook up with him even though you *know* you shouldn't but he wears you down, showing up only to keep you up all night. He disrespects you and makes you feel like crap. And then he just will NOT. STOP. TEXTING! He's the worst. Sometimes guilt likes to come over and tell me a really sweet bedtime story called "You Suck," and it's about how once upon a time there was an incompetent mom named Kristina, and the story never, ever ends.

I want my kids to have better boundaries with their guilt than I have had with mine, so I try to offer alternative narratives whenever their guilt starts telling them a negative story about who they are.

One day, I picked up my then sixth grader from school, and as she got in the car, she immediately started sobbing.

"Matea, what's wrong?"

"I got a really bad grade on my math test. REALLY bad! And I feel so guilty about it!"

Math. The subject she'd been getting all A's in. Personally, I blame the existence of math on Satan, but my daughter is one of those weird humans who actually speaks the language of math really well. Yet here she was with a bad grade and so disappointed in herself. It was the worst grade she had ever gotten. We chatted about it for a bit, but unfortunately, I was in a rush to get her and her brother to their dad's house for the weekend and our conversation was cut short.

When I got home, I decided to email her. I didn't want her dwelling on this bad grade for the entire weekend.

Dear Matea,

Soooo . . . you got a really bad grade today, and guess what? I'm proud of you!

I'm proud that you took complete responsibility for it without making any excuses.

I'm proud that you decided to email your teacher and ask for help.

I'm proud that you're a really good, kind person because that is much more important to me than grades will ever be.

However, a really bad grade does require a consequence, so here is what I expect you to do:

1. Let it go! It's nothing to feel guilty about. I know you're really upset, but don't let one bad grade ruin your day. A year from now, you won't even remember this. Plus feeling like a loser has never helped anyone thrive in life.

2. Keep in mind that one bad grade doesn't mean you're a bad math student. And it definitely doesn't mean you're not smart. It's so easy for us to focus on the one time we fail instead of the many times we succeed. You'll fail again at times. Maybe not at math. Maybe not even at anything that has to do with school. But you'll fail again in life, and you know what that means? That means you're a human! (Which is good, because I was kind of hoping for a human when I gave birth to you. After 33 hours of labor, I would have been really bummed if the doctor handed me a turtle. Nothing against turtles.)

3. Ask yourself, "What can I learn from this?" Failure can actually be a good thing, but only if we choose to learn something from it.

I love you, sweetheart! Now go deal with those three consequences I gave you, OR ELSE!

Love you,
Mom

She wrote back telling me how much better that email made her feel. In that moment, though, I realized that I don't extend the same grace to myself that I give to my children.

I try to parent my kids to look at failure as a lesson, not a verdict; to be patient and forgiving not only of others but of themselves, too; and yet I can't seem to take my own lectures to heart.

There are times when I swear that parenting will send me to the loony bin quicker than my youngest can utter "But why?" for the 584th time today. And then there are other times when I feel like parenting is healing me. Considering how insane I feel most days as I try to survive the circus I've created, it might be weird to admit this, but I actually find parenting therapeutic. I'm giving my kids what I needed, and sometimes what I still need.

In the case of Matea's math test, I gave my daughter permission to fail, I gave her grace, and I gave her my faith in her. I'm learning that if my child deserves those things from me, then I don't deserve any less. One time when Luka was seven, he got so upset and frustrated with himself about something he had done, and I wasn't happy with the way I was handling his frustration. So I looked at him and said, "Listen, you've never been seven before. And I've never been a parent to a seven-year-old before. So let's learn together." You don't expect a seven-year-old to know how to do certain things the very first time around. If it's your first time parenting in a certain situation, give yourself the same grace you're giving your child. Let yourself mess up without beating yourself up for it.

Beating myself up sometimes actually feels easier than cutting myself a break. Easier because it's more familiar and what is familiar tends to feel more comfortable, even when it's bad for us.

But always just doing what is easy and comfortable (even when it's unhealthy) is not the example I want to set for my children. And I know they're learning much more from how they see me live my life and how much grace I give myself than they will ever learn from any lecture I preach at them. If I want to raise kids who can deal with mistakes in a healthy way, I have to lead by example. And that's really freaking annoying sometimes. Can't we just rent good examples for our kids so that we don't have to work so hard? Is that an option? Not asking for a friend.

I was given a beautiful example of grace and perspective shortly after my divorce. In the wake of the drama, desperation, and guilt that accompanied my divorce, I became so depressed I could barely even recognize myself anymore. Raising young children is hard enough when everything is going well. But in that low moment, nothing in my life was going well. Luckily, a dear friend discovered a way for me to get free therapy sessions from some psychology students who needed to log treatment hours in order to graduate. One particularly hard day, I was telling my therapist how I felt like I'd become a really bad mom.

"I'm crap. I really am. I'm a big pile of crap and my children deserve so much better than me. This is not the kind of mom I thought I'd be. This is not the kind of mom I *used* to be."

The therapist asked me for some examples. "Be specific. I want to understand what makes you such a horrible mom now in comparison to when you first became a mom."

"Well, before my divorce, I used to cook these amazing meals from scratch for my kids, and now so many days I just make mac and cheese out of a box. And before my divorce, I used to take my children to fun places. We went everywhere, to museums and parks, and now I'm so depressed that I just stick my kids in front of the TV, sometimes for hours, while I hide away from them and cry like the sucky mom that I am."

I went on and on with these examples, sure that my therapist was fully judging my deterioration as a mother.

Once I finished, the therapist leaned in, looked at me so genuinely, and said, "Wow, Kristina. You are an amazing mom!" With not a hint of sarcasm in his tone, he continued, "You are at your rock bottom, yet you still make sure that the needs of your children are met. You still take the time to go buy that box of pasta and boil it and make sure it's cooled down enough for them to enjoy it. You are so depressed, but you don't want your children seeing you like that all the time and worrying about you, so you turn on their favorite cartoons so that they can laugh and enjoy themselves while you hide and cry by yourself. That is so selfless."

The therapist took every single bad thing I said about myself and turned it around completely. He took every insult I had thrown at myself and transformed each one into a compliment. This conversation was nothing short of life changing for me. I needed to learn to do that for myself, to switch my perspective and tell my critical inner voice to sit down and shut up. (But, you know, nicely. With a compassionate, nonjudgmental, licensed-counselor voice. That I'm obviously still working on.)

It is an act of love to listen to a sad story someone is telling about themselves and then help them spin it so it's maybe a little less sad and a little more meaningful. It can be both simple and profound to step up and be someone's emotional PR rep. As much as you might want to, you can't fix someone else's problems for them and it doesn't make anyone feel better to hear that their situation isn't as bad as it seems, so resist the misguided impulse to recast their reality for them that way. But just listening without judgment and reframing their narrative with compassion is one of the kindest things you can do for your children, your spouse, and especially yourself.

The grace and kindness my therapist gave me that day helped me learn something else as well: I have worried that if I praised my children too much for small accomplishments, I would set their standards too low and accidentally raise brats who wouldn't strive to live up to their full potential. What I realized instead is that without praise for the small things, there's no motivation to get past the small and try to accomplish the big. Giving our kids a chance to see they've made us proud is powerful; it puts the wind in their sails.

We don't mean to, but many of us parents tend to notice the bad in our kids. We're scared we'll raise lazy, entitled, mean humans, so we're constantly on the lookout, making sure we catch them every time they do something bad so that we can nip that behavior in the bud. And, yes, consequences for bad behavior are important. But what if we decided to be just as vigilant, if not more, about noticing what our kids are doing right—even small things—and praising them for that, too? And what if we extended that to ourselves and looked not just at the areas that need improvement but fully appreciated every facet of our lives where we shine?

Let's be honest. We are responsible for a ridiculous number of things. We handle everyone's schedules, we make sure the doctor and dentist appointments are made, and we get our kids to those appointments on time (sort of). We make sure our family is nourished, physically and emotionally. We are the comforters, the conflict-resolution gurus, the therapists, the potty trainers, the storytellers, the teachers, the chefs, the sanitary engineers, and the CEOs of our households. With so many things on our plates and so much constantly racing through our minds, it's easy to slip into autopilot parenting mode. We might as well be pressing the replay button on our words, like the most disappointing action figure ever, complete with the lamest set of prerecorded phrases: "Please have another bite." "Please put your shoes on." "Please finish your homework." Parenting can feel like a monotonous cycle; it's the same thing over and over. By the end of the day, we're drained from all we've managed to do and yet we feel like we've accomplished nothing.

But consider for a moment what would really happen if you disappeared from your life. How many things would fall apart or go undone? Those little things you spend your day doing seem little only because we're not in the habit of giving ourselves credit for them—as meaningful work. In reality, we are so freaking important and needed, even our smallest contributions are vital to keeping our families on track. But instead of marveling at all the minor miracles we perform, we lie in bed at night wide awake, feeling guilty, beating ourselves up for the one thing we overlooked. The emotional burden of the guilt we shoulder is probably more exhausting than the actual endless everyday parenting tasks we accomplish. Now, I'm no sleep expert, but here's a tip I have found that works well: give yourself more credit than criticism, more grace than judgment, and you'll fall asleep more peacefully.

I invited a few friends over once to make a video with me, and I asked them to share with me some of the worst things they tell themselves throughout the day. One said, "I tell myself that I'm lazy and a pig." Another said, "I'm constantly telling myself that I'll never lose this weight I've gained." Another called herself a selfish liar. Another admitted, "I tell myself almost on a weekly basis, if not daily, that I'm just not a good enough mother to my kids." When I pressed them to really think about those statements and weigh them against reality, each woman agreed that there wasn't much truth there. And yet after repeating those insults over and over again, they had unintentionally and unconsciously made them a part of their identity. It's amazing how much of our guilt is built upon lies. After each woman was done sharing her negative thoughts, I surprised them by pulling out a childhood picture of each of them. I asked them to look at that little girl in the picture and tell her the same words that they had been telling themselves. Could they tell that little girl she was a lazy pig or not good enough?

Not one of them could do it. They didn't have the heart to say those cruel words to a younger version of themselves, but they had no problem being their own worst bully now. As they realized how extreme the negativity they'd been carrying about themselves was, it was impossible not to get emotional. I urge everyone to try this powerful exercise. In fact, I've recently talked to my older kids about this and made sure they each have a childhood picture up in their bedrooms. I want them to learn to talk to themselves with kindness, too. Somehow, looking at a childhood photo of ourselves makes us realize how much love and care we need and deserve.

The truth is that we're hard on ourselves because we hate falling short of our own expectations. We hate that we struggle with this parenting thing in a way we hadn't predicted we would before we had kids. That's the whole reason we feel unnecessary guilt, isn't it? We feel guilty because we feel like we're failing. We feel like we're failing because we're not living up to our expectations. But the only reason we're not living up to them is because those expectations were completely ridiculous, semiabusive, and unrealistic in the first place! So we obviously need to set some new expectations. Give this some thought: it would break your child's heart to hear anyone speak to their mommy the way you speak to yourself.

Whenever I'm feeling like a terrible person or a terrible parent, it's usually not because I'm truly terrible but *because I am telling myself a bad story about me.* Stories are powerful things. Tell yourself a story often enough, and it can start to shape your reality.

So the story I try to tell myself now is this: I am someone who is extraordinary in some ways and at some times, but very average most of the time. Rather than lying in bed at night feeling guilty about all the things I didn't accomplish (which basically means feeling guilty that I'm not a robot who can stay alert twenty-four hours a day while perfectly executing all 2,547 things on her to-do list), I try to switch my mind-set and do the opposite. I wipe off the guilt mascara one layer at a time and I start thinking about all the things I did accomplish: My kids have been fed and loved today. My house is still standing. I returned one phone call. I paid a bill. I didn't die. I peed. (Occasionally even in private! Bonus points for that.)

Resetting my expectations to align with a more realistic bar acknowledges that I'm winging this whole be-a-good-human thing as best I can. It means accepting that sometimes I will screw up. I will make mistakes. I will be a terrible example for my children at times. But continually beating myself up accomplishes nothing good. There's no valedictorian in parenting. Being average is completely acceptable. We're not failing. We're learning! Why beat ourselves up for learning? That's something to be proud of! Plus every day is a second chance to suck at life less. (Can I get an amen?) So let's just love our families fiercely and try not to completely lose our minds.*

—————

*Semilosing our minds is expected and totally normal.

Six

I Didn't Tell

The first time was when I was five. He was a clean-cut, nice-looking grandpa type who, after watching us flail around a bit, had stepped in to give my friend and me some pointers on how to swim. But he wasn't teaching me to swim; he was putting his hand inside my bathing suit and occasionally even sticking his finger inside of me. The only details that stand out vividly are the feeling of his hand sliding under my bathing suit bottom and the sound of the fans that were running full blast at the indoor pools. To this day the sound of a loud fan makes me feel anxious. Small. Used.

I didn't tell. I didn't tell a single soul, not even my mom.

For years after that incident at the public pool, I had a recurring nightmare: I'm lying on a table in a small dark room. There is no other furniture in the room. There are no windows, no decorations. The walls are bare and dark gray. I'm not sure if I'm tied down or not, but I'm unable to move. I'm five or six or seven years old, whatever age I was each time this nightmare came back to haunt me, and grown men are taking turns, one by one, entering the room and touching my private parts. Though I'm a little older each time this nightmare occurs, the state of my helplessness remains the same. I never seem to outgrow my inability to fight back or even speak up.

If I woke up from the nightmare and anyone asked why I was crying, I would lie. "I was being chased by the big, bad wolf." At the time, it didn't seem like there was any other option but to lie. How could I ever tell the truth about something so shameful? I was a bad girl for letting someone touch me like that in real life and I was a bad girl for continuing to have those thoughts in my head for years after.

The event at the swimming pool haunted me and, instead of fading with time, intruded on my thoughts more and more as I approached puberty. My mom could tell something was wrong, and when I was twelve or thirteen years old, she gently remarked one afternoon that I hadn't seemed like myself lately and asked if there was anything I wanted to talk about. Finally, tearfully, I told her what the man in the pool had done. We were sitting on her bed and she wrapped me up in her arms and said the words I needed so badly to hear: "It wasn't your fault. I'm so sorry that happened to you." I didn't remember his name and I couldn't even describe his face so there was nothing we could do to get justice, but just sharing the secret I had been carrying all those years made me feel like I could finally breathe again. And the nightmares stopped.

WHEN I WAS in my midtwenties, a friend of mine encouraged me to sign up for an acting class in Los Angeles. "Your college degree is in theater," she said, "and you never know what types of connections you might build. I know you're going through a lot right now, but I think it'd be good for you."

I was going through a lot, indeed. I had two children, one barely three years old and the other eighteen months, and I had just decided to leave my marriage. I was sleeping on the sofa in the apartment I still shared with my not-yet-official ex, because I hadn't figured out where else I could go or how I'd pay for it with no savings of my own. But I took my friend's advice anyway and signed up for an acting class that became vital to my survival: it was a two-hour weekly escape from the stress of my daily life as a soon-to-be-divorced stay-at-home mom with an uncertain future.

On the last day of class, the students performed for a few industry professionals. I did a comedic scene and had so much fun letting go of the drama in my personal life and wearing someone else's skin for a while.

I didn't expect anything to come of the class, but a few days after our performance, one of the talent managers who had attended got in touch to say that he thought I had enough talent to "make it in this business." I was flattered and hopeful that maybe if I could actually book some acting work, postdivorce life would seem a bit easier, at least financially.

My new talent manager and I met up a few times to discuss the plan for my career, and I signed a lengthy contract. When we interacted, he was nothing but professional. No flirting. No inappropriate looks or conversations. He was the perfect gentleman.

Then one evening, we had a meeting at a fancy high-rise building in Los Angeles. By the time we were finished, it was dark outside. As we left the building, he asked me if I could drop him off at a restaurant for a dinner meeting he had scheduled. He'd taken a taxi to our meeting and his next destination was on my way home, so I didn't mind giving him a lift. We got in my car and continued our business-related conversation as we started off across town.

We had gotten stuck in the typical, annoying Los Angeles traffic when—completely out of the blue—he reached over, placed his hand on my inner thigh, and then grabbed my crotch. Surprised and disgusted, I screamed, "What are you doing?! Stop!" I tried to pull his hand off me, but he was stronger and bigger and free, while I was still trying to safely control a car, unable to pull over with all the other cars surrounding me. By now, his seat belt was off and he was leaning in close to me, both hands groping and massaging me. I pushed back against his chest and yelled, "We're going to get into a car accident! Get off of me now!" But he didn't seem fazed. He acted as if he owned me, like I was just a body with no voice, no say, no feelings. There was no fear or shame in his voice as he arrogantly and very calmly whispered in my ear, "You're enjoying it. You know you are."

The entire ordeal didn't last more than a few minutes, though it felt like time had slowed down. Finally, I found a place to pull over and I threw the car into park. I told him to get out, and thankfully, he obliged. I don't know what I would have done if he'd refused; I'd never felt more powerless as an adult. I felt like garbage. I felt empty. Numb. Small. Used.

As I drove off, my entire body was shaking. What had just happened? And why in the world did he think that was okay? Could I have done more to stop him? Thank goodness he wasn't the one driving the car. He could have taken me somewhere and raped me! Did I say or do something in the previous few weeks to make him think I wanted this? What. Just. Happened.

I drove back to that apartment I still shared with my first husband, walked in . . . and said nothing. The next morning, I sat down and drafted a letter to my manager stating that I was ending our business contract due to this sexual assault. I wanted the words "sexual assault" in writing. I wanted him to know that I wasn't oblivious to what had happened and that I understood how serious it was. I wanted him to know that, no, I hadn't enjoyed it. I didn't want it! I mailed the letter a day later and then drove to the police station. I was determined to report this. It *had* to be reported. He committed a crime! In the parking lot at the police station, as I started to reach for the door handle of my car, my body froze while my mind raced.

It's going to be my word against his. I can't prove it. And I'm about to leave my husband. Could this affect my divorce proceedings? What if my soon-to-be ex accuses me of having an affair with this guy? Could I lose custody of my kids? And now that I know how arrogant and brash this man is, what else is he capable of? What might he do to retaliate? He has money. He has power. I have nothing. Nothing except for my word. Is my word enough?

I sat in front of the police station for over an hour. And then I drove away. I didn't tell.

I didn't tell my friends or family. I didn't tell anyone. I was embarrassed that I had even put myself in a situation where I was alone in a car with a man I barely knew. I was embarrassed that I didn't punch him or somehow have the strength to push him off of me. And, after some time, I was embarrassed that I hadn't reported it.

If you asked those closest to me to describe me, you'd hear "strong" and "outspoken" and "brave" and "doesn't put up with crap." And they'd be right. I am all of those things. Women like me don't let someone get away with abuse, assault, or demeaning us. Never. Except sometimes we do. And sometimes the reasons we do are so complex and confusing that we can't fully make sense of them.

I wish I had immediately told a friend. I wish I had asked that friend to take me to the police station, make me get out of the car, hold my hand, and remind me as many times as necessary that my body and my dignity and the truth are worth more than his money and his power and anyone's doubts.

I'd like to tell you that my experiences are uncommon, but they're not. Over the years, especially since I started posting videos online, women of all ages have shared their pain with me. Sometimes the pain is decades old and still uncomfortable to speak about. Sometimes I'm the first person they've told. And every time someone shares a story like that, I want to grab hold of my children and never let them go. But I can't protect them from all the evil in this world. I can, however, teach them to speak up.

(If you're wondering why I won't name the manager who assaulted me, it's only because he has one of the most generic names of all time, a name that I'm sure belongs to at least one other blameless, perfectly lovely talent manager in Los Angeles, and I don't want to hurt anyone by accident.)

Last year, I posted a screenshot of a vulgar comment that a man had left on my Facebook page. I get inappropriate sexual comments all the time; every woman does, and when you're a public figure, you receive even more. My standard response: ignore, delete, block. But this particular guy had been posting vulgar comments on my videos for months, and every time I'd block him, he'd pop back up with a new profile. I'd had enough.

So I took a screenshot of his newest contribution and posted it to my Instagram feed with the hashtag #outthem in the caption. I didn't black out his name or profile picture; I just shared what he'd already thought was a perfectly acceptable thing to say to me publicly.

I expected backlash from other obnoxious men who think women should take sexual harassment as a compliment, but most of the replies I got from men were along the lines of "I hate guys like this douchebag. They give all of us a bad name."

To my great surprise, the backlash came from a few women:

> His post is not alright, but when you put him on blast like this, that's not alright either. I know you can be better than this. You have chosen to be an example to others, to be someone to follow, and this is how you address the situation?

> You're always talking about kindness. How is it kind to expose him like this?

> Some guys just say the wrong thing when they're flirting because they get nervous around a girl they find pretty.

These *women* were upset I had outed this man. Women, in the year 2019, were rallying to support a sexual harasser. Why? Why do some women make so many excuses for men's bad behavior? Because we've all been brainwashed to think that sexual harassment is shameful and should be kept private.

One of the reasons I didn't say anything when I was molested at the age of five was because I was embarrassed by what had happened. But what did I have to be embarrassed about? It wasn't my fault. The only person who should have been embarrassed by his behavior was the man who had violated me. Why was I carrying around his shame for him? Why are women always running around picking up men's shame like dirty socks?

We are taught from girlhood to be nice and to protect other people's feelings, even at the expense of our own well-being. We learn, by example, that we are supposed to cater to everyone else around us. We cater to the men in our lives. We cater to our children. We cater to our friends. We cater to strangers. Does everyone have what they need? Is everyone feeling good and doing great? I address the concerns of others without even thinking, as automatically as a reflex, but when it comes to taking care of myself I have to pause and remember to ask myself, *Wait, do I have everything I need? Am I feeling good and doing great?*

I try my best to be empathetic and think about what might be happening in someone else's life that could be influencing their behavior, but even my empathy must have its boundaries. Another person crosses that boundary when their words or actions threaten mine or anyone else's physical or emotional safety. Why are we more concerned with protecting the reputation of jerks who are sexually harassing women than with making sure every single woman feels safe and respected?

We forget to differentiate between being nice and being kind. But they are not interchangeable. According to the dictionary, "nice" is defined as "pleasing; agreeable; delightful." Nice is sitting quietly with your legs crossed at the ankles. Nice is "He didn't mean it." Nice is "You should just take it as a compliment." In other words, being nice is about superficially behaving in a way that makes other people feel comfortable.

Kindness, on the other hand, is defined as "having, showing, or proceeding from benevolence." There is strength in kindness. Kindness comes from a deeper place of morals and values, of wanting to do the right thing because ultimately it betters the world. Kindness is looking out for other humans by doing what might make some people or myself uncomfortable in the short term, like exposing sexist, derogatory pigs for what they are. I'm kind to the world when I push back against a culture that normalizes inappropriate behavior. Because unsolicited, explicit sexual advances are not awkward flirting; they are about power and intimidation. I aim to set an important and valuable example when I show other women that we don't have to take this crap silently.

One of the young women I hope I'm reaching is my own daughter, who I hope will come of age with a pretty high standard for what she should tolerate and how she deserves to be treated.

At my first-ever parent-teacher conference for Matea, her kindergarten teacher, Mrs. Miller, informed me that my daughter was a wonderful, bright student, but she was having one big issue with her. I braced myself.

"During recess, Matea really likes to play on the swing set. But frequently, another student will run up and grab the swing from her just before Matea sits down, and whenever this happens Matea just looks down or walks away and I'm worried that she's not standing up for herself."

Mrs. Miller went on to explain that one day she'd taken Matea by the hand, walked her back to the swings, and told her she needed to tell the boy who'd cut her off, "I was here first, and you can have it after I'm done."

The fact that this amazing person was looking out for my daughter when I wasn't there—during recess, no less, her only break during the whole workday—and teaching her such important lessons made me tear up with gratitude. But how had I missed this? Had I inadvertently bought into the seemingly default rule for girls in our society, that asking for what they want is somehow considered rude? I needed to pay closer attention to the way my daughter interacted with other kids and make a point of gently challenging her in the moments I witnessed those sneaky, toxic messages taking hold, because the world won't, and there won't always be a Mrs. Miller around to step in and model a gentle but firm touch for her.

The harmful messages the world has for our daughters about who and what and how they should be have been in the spotlight the past few years, but the world has plenty of nonsense to tell our sons, too.

You know how people will post a picture of a man making scrambled eggs for breakfast for his child and everyone on the internet loses their fricking minds? The comments section will explode with gushing praise like "What an amazing father. This post needs to go viral," and "He is the BEST dad," and "Oh my gosh, he is so sexy! A man who makes breakfast for his kid? HOT."

Seriously? All a father has to do is make breakfast for his child and he's sexy? Or play with his kid or do the laundry or braid his daughter's hair? Why do we perpetuate the assumption that men aren't capable of basic parenting? What an insult to men. Honestly, I wouldn't have such a problem with posts like this if we made an equal fuss over the million little things women do every day to take care of our children. But have you ever seen someone comment "Wow. That is SO attractive. This should go viral!" when someone posts a photo of a mother tucking her own child into bed? Nope. It shouldn't be seen as extraordinary for a father to lovingly care for his own children.

The greatest insult our society dumps on men, though, is the old adage "Boys will be boys." As a mother raising two boys, that saying, frankly, pisses me off. "Boys will be boys" implies that men simply can't help how they think or speak or act. "Boys will be boys," with the help of countless movies and commercials, tells us that men think with their penises and can't be expected to control themselves. But having no self-control implies that a person is weak, and since when do men want to be seen as weak? "Boys will be boys" says, "Well, yeah, they're male, so it's no surprise they're acting immaturely; it's in their nature."

My sons (and everyone else's, too) were born with a brain and a heart, the ability to make choices, and the power to treat fellow human beings, male or female, appropriately and respectfully. Even in private. Even when no one is watching or listening. Even when there's no chance of getting caught. To expect or accept anything less from my boys would be disrespectful and degrading to their characters, their potential.

Instead of simply teaching our sons that girls are meant to be protected, we need to get them excited about helping to create a world where girls don't have to be afraid anymore. We need to make it very clear to our sons that they are not just doing women a favor by standing up against sexism. They are actually fighting for a stronger, smarter, kinder world, one that is possible only if women are treated equally. Let's raise incredible guys who will know their worth as decent, responsible men and capable, involved, loving dads. Raising real men starts in our homes. It starts with us.

YEARS AGO, I watched my four-year-old daughter playing in the living room. She was sassy and bold, yet kind and sensitive; she was opinionated yet open-minded. And so brave. So very brave. And I thought: *I want to be like her when I grow up.*

Since then, whenever I find myself in a dilemma, I ask myself this question: *If my daughter faces this situation someday, how would I want her to handle it?* Somehow the answer is always clearer when I try to channel my daughter. Because I want better for her than I've ever wanted for myself.

If I could go back and ask that question at all the moments in my life when I found myself stuck in scary situations, I would have handled them better. And though the pain might still be there, the healing would have come easier and more quickly, because at least I would have been confident in my own response, clear about what was within my power and what was out of my control.

As parents, it comes so naturally for us to love our children and want the absolute best for them, but it's not as natural to want that same extraordinary goodness for ourselves. It's easier for me to speak up for myself now that I'm a parent, because every time I shine a light on evil and injustice, I'm not just doing it for myself; I'm doing it for my kids. It's easier for me to let go of shame and guilt and stop beating myself up over the couldas and shouldas, because I don't want my children to carry those burdens, and I know they are watching and listening closely.

We need to teach our children that when another human being is treated as less than, standing by silently isn't neutral; it's destructive. Instilling those values requires honest communication from a young age, and we shouldn't wait until our children are grown to teach them about equality and respect. Sitting them down for a serious talk every once in a while is useless. The serious talk needs to be an ongoing two-way conversation in which we help them find their own words, so that when the time comes to speak up, they aren't silent.

Whether we're prepared for the responsibility or not, we are the most powerful influence on what the future of this world holds. We are not just raising our kids. We are raising someone's future spouse, possibly someone's parent, someone's employee, someone's boss, someone's neighbor, someone's closest, most trustworthy friend.

It starts with us. And I, for one, am done being silent.

Seven

Cynicism Interrupted

When I was single again, it seemed like everyone in my life was trying to set me up with their friend or doctor or old college roommate. One birthday, I got a gift card from a friend for a beauty salon, and while I was lying on a bed, legs spread-eagle, getting a bikini wax, the nice woman ripping hair from my lady parts started telling me about her single brother who was really good with kids. (Some unsolicited advice for anyone whose job requires them to work near a vagina: work might not be the best place to talk to your clients about how romantic and sweet your brother is.)

It was as if the entire world were determined to find me a man. I guess that's the cool, movielike thing to do: set the single mom up with her Prince Charming. Or maybe people just saw me as their charity case, and getting me a date was the one good deed they felt sure they could reasonably accomplish.

But I wasn't looking for Prince Charming. I wasn't even look-ing for his valet. Having a relationship seemed like more work than I wanted to heap onto my already overflowing plate. No man was going to be able to handle my chaotic life.

I was so cynical after my divorce that I didn't believe any mar-ried people were genuinely happy together. Couples would come into the restaurant where I worked to celebrate their anniversa-ries and I'd congratulate them with the required-to-ensure-a-good-tip "Wow, twenty years! That's amazing! So happy for you!" But when I finished pouring their champagne, I'd head back to the kitchen thinking, *Twenty years?! Those two must be SO miser-able.* I just assumed all long-term relationships sucked and that any duos who appeared joyful were faking it.

Nevertheless, out on some dates I went. Occasionally. But most of the time, within the first fifteen minutes, I regretted agreeing to go out. I regretted showering for the date. (Shower-ing is a luxury when you're a single mom to two very young kids. You can't waste that kind of time, or water, for just a mediocre date.) I regretted asking a friend to watch my kids so I could waste some poor guy's time. Or if it was the weekend, I regretted not using the hour lunch break between my two jobs to take a nap or do something for myself—something, anything, that didn't include a pointless date.

It's not that there was anything wrong with these guys. I met an ER doctor who humored my requests for stories about the strangest things he'd pulled out of people. He was handsome and kind and what many women would have described as "a great catch." Another guy seemed perfectly lovely until I learned about his infatuation with and complete commitment to the raw food diet, which was a problem because carbs are one of my love languages. And with yet another guy, I'm convinced we could have been lifelong best friends if we had just avoided complicating that by trying to date.

I just wasn't in a place where I could see myself fully committing to anyone. I wasn't into the idea of a boyfriend. I wasn't into the idea of love. I was perfectly content for the only romance in my life to be my committed relationship with cynicism, and I didn't want to allow anyone to get in the way of that.

One day at the restaurant, my coworker Daniela and I were planning an evening out at a karaoke bar. We were ironing out the details when Philip, an interim manager, passed by, so we invited him to come along.

Everyone liked Philip. He'd been with us for only about six months, taking over while the owners worked on a new restaurant, which was under construction. But he'd quickly won over all the staff. He was smart and kind and positive, but not in the nausea-inducing, fake way I was used to seeing "positive" people behave. He was also dependable and reasonable and rational—characteristics most people appreciate, especially in a boss. And he was the best at handling the most annoying customers.

Fine-dining restaurants attract a lot of entitled clientele. I'm not saying everyone who eats fancy food is a monster (I like fancy food and I've been called a monster only once . . . by one of my kids, and that just simply doesn't count), but fancy restaurants do seem to experience a higher concentration of people who'll ask their server to leave the restaurant and walk two blocks to a specialty store to pick up a specific cheese they'd prefer to have grated onto their salad. And because some of the finicky customers were regulars who would drop a thousand dollars every week at the restaurant, we'd comply with even the most outlandish requests. The restaurant was a true establishment, a place where customers wanted and expected special attention, and any alteration to the menu inevitably resulted in complaints from those who missed the way it used to be.

Most of the managers would handle complaints from tables by either blowing them off or comping part of the customers' meals, both of which are a bummer for the server because we lose out on tips. But Philip had this way of changing people's moods. He'd go to a table that had been angry and impossible to please all night, and by the time he left, the diners would be smiling and cracking jokes and complimenting the server who couldn't do anything right just moments earlier.

Everyone liked Philip.

So Daniela and I were happy to invite him to our karaoke night.

The day before the karaoke outing, Philip called my cell phone. He had never called me before. In fact, we had never even spoken outside of work.

"I'm calling because I was thinking that we should grab dinner before karaoke," he said.

"Oh, that sounds great!" I said. "Let me call Daniela and make sure that works for her."

Daniela informed me that she already had dinner plans, so I called Philip back. "Unfortunately, Daniela can't make it to dinner."

"Perfect!" Philip sounded happy. I was perplexed, followed quickly by feeling annoyed. Maybe Philip wasn't such a good guy after all. Maybe he was a big two-faced phony.

"Perfect? Perfect?!? What do you mean 'perfect'? Do you not like Daniela? You don't want to hang out with her? So let me get this straight. You pretend you're fine with her to her face, but then behind her back, you think it's 'perfect' that you don't have to be around her? Listen, she's my friend and I think you're incredibly rude, and I just want you to know—"

As I was going off, standing up for Daniela, Philip interrupted, "Whoa, whoa, whoa. Slow down there. I have nothing against her. Nothing! It's just that when I said I wanted to have dinner with you, I meant *just* you."

I very quickly and awkwardly ended the conversation and called Daniela back, frantically asking why Philip would want to have dinner with *just* me.

"I mean . . . is he suggesting a date? Like, a real date? Does he like me? Like, *like me* like me? More than a friend? Ugh, this is so uncomfortable. I'm just not interested in him in that way. I'm not having dinner with *just* him!"

I'd never thought of Philip in a romantic way. Because America was in the middle of the Great Recession, business had slowed at the restaurant, and so I'd gotten to know him a little better than I might have otherwise, while we chatted during the downtime. The restaurant employed several managers, so I never really felt like he was my boss, and I thought he was a nice guy, the kind of guy I'd want to set up with a really great girl. But *I* wasn't that girl!

The next day I did everything I could to make sure Philip knew our dinner was *not* a date. I put on jeans—my least favorite pair of jeans!—and a loose shirt with no shape whatsoever that had a permanent brown stain on it. (I am 98.2 percent certain the stain was not from my children's fecal matter. Let's just assume it was chocolate.) I didn't worry about how my hair or makeup looked. I drove myself (because if he picked me up, he might think this was a date, which it definitely was not) and spent the whole ride thinking up ways to get out of this dinner if it started feeling like a date.

Philip had chosen a small Vietnamese restaurant called Gingergrass that didn't take reservations, and when we arrived, there was a forty-five-minute wait to be seated, so we decided to get a drink at a wine shop across the street. We wandered through the aisles of crates, sipping our wine and looking to see if they had anything Croatian.

At one point, I glanced up at Philip leaning against the wall with his glass of wine and something in me shifted. I'd never really seen him outside of work and the change in setting allowed me to look at him with fresh eyes. He was talking, but I couldn't hear him anymore. *What is going on?* I thought. *Why do I suddenly feel attracted to this guy?*

Philip had always been warm when we'd spoken at work, but also entirely professional. I'd never gotten a flirtatious vibe from him, which I appreciated given his position; I was starting to realize it might be why I'd never thought of him romantically before. He was going to be leaving soon to manage the new restaurant, so I didn't really have to worry about whether my feelings toward him would affect my position at work, and I trusted his character enough to know that if things got awkward he'd be mature and gracious. I sipped my wine and allowed myself to enjoy the unexpected new feelings I was having in this man's company.

Later that night, as I sat across from Philip at the tiny restaurant, stealing bites of Shaking Beef off his plate with a fork, I felt like myself. And for some strange reason, "myself" didn't feel so complicated or overwhelming when I was around him.

Most people try to sell themselves on first dates, highlighting their best features and trying their hardest to hide their insecurities and failures. But Philip came across as so genuine and comfortable that I managed to bring him fully up-to-date on my dreadful mental state the prior year, the various conflicts with people in my life, the state of my stretch marks, and even the fact that sometimes I pee myself when I laugh.

The dinner ended with my fighting him for the check. We were going to split it because if he paid this would be a date and, despite my new curiosity about him, THIS WAS NOT A DATE!!!

I lost. He won. He paid. But still . . . not a date.

When we met up with Daniela at the karaoke bar after dinner, Philip surprised me again. He'd always struck me as the quiet type, but he performed a shockingly good rendition of George Michael's "Kissing a Fool" in a delicious baritone. I sang a New Kids on the Block song, and then we sang a duet of Elton John and Kiki Dee's "Don't Go Breaking My Heart." (He later saved my name as "Kiki" in his phone, which also happens to be a nickname for Kristina in Croatia.) Over the course of the evening, I went from seeing him as a really nice guy to seeing him as a really nice guy I wanted to make out with.

The THIS IS NOT A DATE evening ended with a kiss and a "Thank you for such a great date, Philip," and a plan for the next date. With each date, I was liking this Philip guy more, and he was getting to me. He was really getting to me.

Philip was different. He wasn't just different from any man I had ever dated; he was different from any man I had ever known. He was selfless, patient, and never once did he pity me. So often we see ourselves in the worst light, and when I looked in the mirror, I still sometimes saw myself as a pathetic, beat-up loser. But when Philip looked at me, he saw a fun-loving girl full of life. Nobody needs a romantic partner to rescue them, and Philip didn't save me; I saved myself. My attitude toward my life had already improved before Philip came along, and I believe I would have had a good and happy life even if we'd never met. But when you're healing after a major depression and learning how to like yourself again, it sure helps to spend time with someone who sees and appreciates the best parts of you.

I didn't start having feelings for Philip because I thought he was perfect. I'm not that naïve. He had and still has plenty of things to work on. (He approved that last sentence.) And I have plenty of things to work on also. (I approve that last sentence.) Philip drew me in because he's as brutally honest and open about his flaws as I'd been about mine on our first date. And, even more important, he's proactive about working on his character glitches instead of just ignoring them. Now, that's hot!

Here's something I learned along the way: pay attention to whether a behavior is a pattern or an event. We all have really bad days, and we all do stupid things and hurt people. We just do. And if what's getting under your skin is a negative event—meaning the behavior is out of character—then dip into your supply of grace and understanding, talk it out, and let it go. It's what you'd want in return. But if what's causing you pain is part of a negative pattern, if it's something that keeps happening and no effort is put toward remedying the behavior, well, then you have a pretty grim decision to make: stay or walk away. (Walk away!)

The pattern (not an event) with Philip has always been that he genuinely respects me, is willing to make sacrifices for me, pays attention to what I need or want or like, and goes out of his way to show me he cares. I have happily embraced those positive patterns.

When we were sure our feelings for each other were real, we requested a meeting with the other managers at the restaurant to let them know that we had started dating. Since Philip was just an interim manager who was leaving within weeks to manage a different restaurant, and because the other managers trusted both of us to be completely professional, they were fine with us dating. In fact, they were ecstatic. The single mom everyone wanted to set up was finally seeing someone! And not just someone, but a really nice guy who everyone respected.

After a while, when I was secure in my feelings for him, I introduced Philip to my children. We never showed any affection in front of them—no flirting, not even holding hands. This was important to me. I didn't want my children to bond with him as some type of fatherly figure, just in case things didn't work out with us. Breakups are hard enough for adults, and we actually have the capacity and insight to understand why things don't always work out, to deal with sadness or rejection. Children bond so fast, and any change in a kid's life is a big change; they aren't equipped to handle all that emotional baggage and they shouldn't have to. I wasn't willing to risk my kids feeling abandoned if this seemingly great relationship didn't last. They had already dealt with the pain and confusion of their parents divorcing. Since I had as many good male friends in my life as female friends, it was easy to introduce Philip to my children as just another friend of mine.

A few months after Philip met my kids, I had a particularly rough night. Matea woke up in the middle of the night vomiting. Beans. Pinto beans. Chewed up, swallowed, and then regurgitated all over the carpet. The chaos woke up Luka, who screamed and cried in exhaustion. It was one of those single-mom moments when I thought I would actually go insane. I looked insane, probably smelled insane, and my head was pounding from all the screaming. I was trying to calm down my children and clean up my daughter and the carpet when I thought, *Why would any man sign up for this?*

So naturally I called Philip and woke him up. "Come over. Come over right now. You say you want me, you say you want my life and everything that comes along with it? Then come over now." He was at my apartment in twenty minutes. The kids were still screaming, and I was on all fours on the floor, scrubbing the carpet. I expected a look of shock or disgust, maybe even anger that I had woken him up in the middle of the night for *this*. But instead, without missing a beat, Philip got down on that floor, grabbed the rag out of my hand, and cleaned up my daughter's vomit. Then he tucked my children in and got them to sleep. And then he tucked me in, kissed my forehead, and said, "Yes, I want this. I want every part of it. All three of you."

Despite all of this, there was still a tiny little part of me that would occasionally interrupt our great dates to wonder whether Philip was genuine. Could I really know him? Could I trust who he really seemed to be or how he really felt about me? I was falling in love with him, but resisting commitment with every bone in my body.

I credit Philip's parents for helping me through my ambivalence. They never sat me down and gave me a heartfelt speech or anything, but watching them interact with each other showed me that maybe I was wrong about my conclusion that all married couples eventually end up miserable together. One evening, Philip and I were having dinner with his dad at his parents' home while his mom was at work, and his father looked over at the empty seat where his wife usually sat and said, "I miss her when she's not here." He missed her. After forty years of marriage, he still missed her.

And then one Easter, Philip was on the phone with his mom, who was telling him to go out and buy my kids the big, prepackaged Easter baskets wrapped in cellophane. She would pay him back. Philip told her he'd just buy candy and put the baskets together himself, that it would be cheaper than shelling out for the prepackaged ones. But his mom insisted that the kids had to have the big, cheesy, prepackaged, cellophane-wrapped baskets. She explained that when she was a little girl, she always wanted one of those and her mom would never buy it for her. Philip's dad overheard her phone conversation with Philip, and it was a story he'd never heard before. He immediately went to the store and bought his wife her very first prepackaged, cellophane-wrapped Easter basket.

As I got to know Philip's family, I found it easier to trust his intentions. He wasn't just trying to win me over. He was genuinely a thoughtful, kind man. He had learned how to be this way from his parents.

During one of our dates, and in the middle of another one of my soapbox rants that Philip had grown accustomed to at this point, I mentioned that I think premarital counseling is a joke. Philip was confused.

"Really? I thought you were a big fan of therapy."

"Oh, I am," I replied. "Huge fan! It's just that after people get engaged, they write out their guest lists and go dress shopping and show off their engagement rings to everyone and start planning out centerpieces and blah, blah, blah . . . and by that point, are they really going to call the wedding off if a therapist tells them they might not be right for each other? My guess is most people still go through with the wedding thinking, *We'll figure it out. Our love can conquer all!* Total delusion. Puke.

"Here's what I think people should do: screw premarital counseling and get preengagement counseling! No one should be proposing to anyone until they've sat down with an experienced, licensed marriage and family therapist and laid it all out on the table."

Within a few months of this conversation, Philip stopped by my apartment and told me the same thing he had apparently told his mom about me after our second date: "I want to spend the rest of my life with you. That's my plan. Now, I understand you might not be there yet, but just in case, I think we should see a therapist. I did a lot of research and found an experienced, licensed marriage and family therapist in our area, one who actually specializes in stepfamilies."

I was in. Philip was paying attention to what was important to me and I was willing to put some serious work into breaking down the walls I had built around my heart following my divorce.

In our preengagement therapy, the therapist asked us to write out our mission statement. Just like businesses have mission statements, she suggested we write one for our relationship. She expected a short paragraph. Philip and I turned in six pages. This exercise forced us to look at our relationship not just as a romantic partnership but also as a business partnership. And if we're going to be honest, marriage (or any long-term committed relationship) is like a business in a lot of ways. Yes, romance and intimacy are important, but they're such a small percentage of what living day in and day out in a partnership with someone actually looks like. The adult responsibilities of bills and budgeting and insurance and appointments and errands can make relationships a nightmare if two people aren't on the same page. I realized that if I wouldn't feel comfortable starting a business with the person I was dating, then I shouldn't start a marriage with that person either. In our mission statement, Philip and I covered everything from finances to romance and sex to our spiritual beliefs to what our goals were when it came to our home life and work life and communication and raising children. We wrote and talked and rewrote for days, and it felt like working on a really exciting project with a really great partner.

Our relationship wasn't a perfect, problem-free partnership, though. We argued a lot. Or, more accurately, I argued. I'd get scared, which would cause me to get bitchy. I questioned myself, him, our relationship. I broke up with him four different times. (All short-lived, because deep down inside I knew I'd be an idiot to let him go.)

Truth is, it wasn't until I met Philip that I started to accept that I was worthy of love just as I was. And when you're not used to being genuinely loved just as you are, it takes some time to adjust to the feeling. In the past, I'd always felt like there were parts of myself I needed to hide in order to be loved. But Philip's demeanor had given me permission to get vulnerable from our very first date, and I was finding that vulnerability leads to intimacy. Emotional intimacy. Real intimacy. I was able to give more of myself to Philip, because for the first time, I wasn't living with the fear of being found out and rejected.

Philip modeled a kind of love for me that was patient, deliberate, calm, and self-assured—open and vulnerable, but with boundaries. I once heard someone describe a healthy relationship as one in which someone makes you feel "held and free." That's the way Philip made me feel. And by the time he proposed to me (and then proposed again in front of Luka and Matea, after asking for their permission to marry their mommy), I was finally ready to go all in.

By the time we were ready to get engaged, Philip had left the restaurant business and decided to go back to school to get a master's in accounting and his CPA license. We were going to be paying for our own wedding, and since I was still earning just enough money to make ends meet and he was now in school full time, we had to get really creative and keep wedding costs low. We invited fifty people. I designed my own dress and found someone to make it for a great price. We made our own wedding invitations. Luka drew the cover of the ceremony program. I baked our wedding cake (actually, an enormous brownie sundae, since that was our favorite dessert to share). A friend generously offered to be our photographer. Nothing we did cost very much, yet that day we felt so rich in all the ways that really mattered.

A few weeks before our wedding, Philip decided he wanted to write a book for my kids and surprise them with it at the ceremony. His first draft was his final draft because after he read it to me, I wouldn't allow him to change a single word. He so perfectly captured how much he cared about us, how the way we loved and welcomed him had given him the courage to ask to be part of our family, what joining our family would look like, and how now anytime Luka and Matea needed something or were sad, they'd have "another person to love them."

On our wedding day, in the middle of the ceremony, a blanket was laid on the grass, the minister called my children up for story time, and Philip read to them.

It was the most beautiful part of an unspeakably beautiful day.

WE HUMANS WANT something wonderful, but we're not always willing to hold out for something wonderful. Or we don't think we deserve something wonderful. Because we have broken relationships behind us, we feel like we've already failed at this love thing. We're exhausted and insecure and completely stressed-out by life. So when we meet someone who gives us the attention we've been craving, sometimes we lose all common sense. We turn stupid. All we can focus on is our shock: He loves me! He loves me even though I'm divorced. He loves me even though I'm struggling financially. He loves me even though I have stretch marks and cellulite and chin hairs. He loves me even though my life is full of drama. And he loves me even though I have children— as if our children are baggage that someone would have to put up with. Using "even though" multiple times when justifying why we're dating someone is a good sign that we're probably letting our insecurities call the shots, and they are not qualified for that job.

I know how lonely being a single parent can get. I know you might feel like you're carrying a load that's too heavy for just one person to bear. I know that having someone in your life to help you get through each exhausting day might sound like the best thing ever. But it won't be the best thing ever if you don't choose a true partner.

There are still really good people out there who will love you for the right reasons, love your children for who they are, be willing to clean up their vomit in the middle of the night, kiss you on the forehead, and remind you that they want every part of your chaotic life. And you are deserving of all those things.

No one should ever give in to the impulse to just settle, but once we have children, we lose the right to settle. Partnering with someone who doesn't respect us, or isn't willing to work hard in the relationship, or make sacrifices for the sake of our children, can leave us in a position way more miserable and risky than going it alone. Don't be fooled into thinking that any partner is better than no partner.

The story of my finding love as a single mom and marrying Philip is beautiful. But there are also not-so-beautiful parts of our story that have to be mentioned in order to paint the most honest picture I can paint for you about my marriage. There are stories of disagreements and arguments. There are stories of resentment and selfishness. There are stories of things that shouldn't have been said, promises that weren't kept, weeks of holding grudges, and days where we didn't even really like each other. Relationships require work and patience and forgiveness and listening and not assuming and honesty and empathy and putting our pride aside and kindness and a bunch of other nouns and verbs that can be really, really freakin' challenging at times. Because . . . human. Marrying Philip was the smartest decision I ever made. I adore him and respect him and I'm so grateful for him. But our marriage isn't perfect. It's not supposed to be. Happily ever after is only as happy as the amount of real work we're willing to put into it, even when we don't feel like it. Not settling is a choice we have to make daily, for the rest of our lives. Getting married doesn't mean that the search for love is over. The search for the person to love is over; the search for how to love that person is just beginning.

Eight

As Is

I still remember the night it started. My older sister and I were glued to the television, watching my future husband, Joey McIntyre, and her future husband, Jordan Knight, sing their hearts out in the latest New Kids on the Block music video. At the time, there were only two TV stations in Croatia, and one of them had a budget for only a few hours of programming a day, so catching anything that would remotely interest a preteen was a very rare and special occasion.

As we fawned over the future fathers of our children, their singing was suddenly drowned out by a loud noise—a kind of giant boom I'd only ever heard before in the movies, but much louder, much closer, and much scarier. The next sound I heard was the hurried *thud-thud-thud* of my parents' feet pounding down our wooden staircase. My father carried my little sister in his arms and screamed, "Get down! Get down! Now! Lie down on the floor! Fast!"

The five of us all lay on our living room floor as the terrifying sounds outside continued. My father lifted his head off the floor, just a tiny bit, and quietly said, "There's a war starting. Things will be different now."

It was June 1991, and what would become known as the Croatian War of Independence had just begun. We lived in the city of Osijek, very close to the Serbian border, and those terrifying sounds that shook our home in the night were grenades thrown by the advancing Serbian army. I was twelve years old and suddenly forced to understand the reality of bombs and the safety of basements, and the fact that hatred is real and powerful and can be aimed at you even if you have done nothing wrong.

When I was born, my country was called Yugoslavia. It was made up of six republics: Croatia, Bosnia and Herzegovina, Slovenia, Montenegro, Serbia, and Macedonia. Each republic had its own leaders and governments, kind of like America's states. Yugoslavia began under Communist leadership, but slowly the republics started to pull apart as, one by one, they sought to become democracies. A man named Slobodan Milošević, who was the leader of Serbia, fanned nationalist flames to attack first Slovenia, then Croatia, and then Bosnia and Herzegovina in an effort to create one Great Serbia.

No war is simple, and the Yugoslavian wars are especially complicated. Religion, ethnicity, both world wars, and centuries of power struggles, bloodshed, and atrocities factored into the violence that erupted in the summer of 1991. But what I need you to understand is that the distinction between Croatians and Serbs wasn't one that felt especially significant to me as a child.

My grandparents were Croatian, but for my entire childhood,

they lived in Serbia, in a little house about an hour and a half away from my hometown. Visiting them didn't feel any different than it would if you lived in New Hampshire and visited family in Vermont. The Serbian and Croatian languages are very similar, so native speakers understand one another easily. There were kids my age in my grandmother's neighborhood, and we spent countless afternoons playing together and climbing trees. So many of my fondest childhood memories took place in Serbia.

When the war started, my parents sent me to my grandmother's house for a few weeks to get me away from all the violence. One afternoon, I saw one of my friends outside and said hello. He didn't respond. He wouldn't even look at me. I ran, upset, to my grandmother and asked her, "Why won't he talk to me?" My grandmother looked at me with sad eyes and said simply, "Because he's Serbian and you're Croatian and there's a war." I had never before experienced rejection based solely on where I was born.

I couldn't understand why people who'd been friends for years were suddenly supposed to hate one another. In the end, tensions became so volatile that my grandparents quickly left Serbia and later sold their house through a series of phone calls without even going back in person to pick up all of their belongings.

Over the course of the war, so many homes and businesses were damaged and then repaired that my city could not produce enough glass to fulfill the demands. When a piece of shrapnel tore a hole through my bedroom window (thankfully no one was home), we repaired it with duct tape and plastic sheeting because there was just no glass left to buy. The window stayed that way for years. A sweet little town nearby called Vukovar was shelled so heavily that it all but disappeared.

War isn't the way it seems in movies. There are days when you hear the sound of sirens, not unlike police cars, and run to the nearest basement, where you wait and pray. The bombs fall nonstop for a certain number of days in a row. But then they stop. For days, weeks, sometimes even months. Things calm down and routines of ordinary life resume and things go back to, if not normal, then something that quickly comes to feel normal. A new normal. Stores open up again for a bit and you go shopping and classes resume at school. I remember seeing tanks and soldiers around my city and being scared at first. And then . . . I got used to it. Humans adapt so quickly and can adapt to almost anything. Life goes on. Until the sirens start up again.

Unlike so many of our dearest friends, my family was able to make it out of Croatia. My father was an expert in East European and missions studies and had built a reputation as an academic speaker. He'd been to the United States several times before to give presentations and to teach courses at seminaries and universities across the country. When I was fourteen years old, my dad was offered a job in the United States, so we packed up and moved to a small town north of Boston.

If you think being a teenager is hard, try being one in a foreign country where your high school English teacher is having you read an abbreviated version of every assigned novel. It was humiliating to pull out my picture-book versions of *A Tale of Two Cities* and *To Kill a Mockingbird* in front of my classmates. One time I was asked to read aloud from our textbook in science class. I was confused as to why everyone was laughing, until the teacher stopped me to point out the correct pronunciation of the word I'd just read wrong at least half a dozen times. It was "organisms." Not "orgasms."

America was completely disorienting at first. I couldn't get used to how bright it was at night. In Croatia, nighttime was dark. But America was lit up by bright billboards, streetlights, and signs for stores that stayed open twenty-four hours a day. How could people work twenty-four hours a day? When did they sleep? In Croatia at the time, most stores closed for lunch and then reopened for a few hours in the afternoon, then closed again in time for dinner.

Just the idea that you could drive up to a little box attached to a little building, tell a voice coming through a machine what food you wanted to eat, and then, moments later, be handed that food in a bag through a window just around the corner blew my mind. Drive-throughs felt just one step away from the kind of thing you'd see on *Star Trek*.

I remember going to a Toys"R"Us store for the first time and being overwhelmed. Not only were there more dolls than I'd ever seen, but I couldn't process all of their outfits and shoes and hair clips and furniture and accessories. In America, a doll could have more than I, a human, had ever owned.

I didn't have the cool clothes, I didn't understand the American sayings or American culture, so I got made fun of at school. But I felt like I couldn't complain, because my friends back home were dealing with so much worse than teasing. In Croatia, my friends worried whether their homes would still be standing after the next air raid, or if their dad, who was fighting for his country, would survive the next battle. Here, my friends complained when their mothers shrank their favorite sweater in the dryer or when a concert was scheduled for the same night as the school dance.

Humans adapt to the good just as quickly and easily as we adapt to the bad, so it wasn't long before American excess that shocked me when I first arrived became something I took for granted. But when I caught myself actually enjoying my new life, I struggled with survivor's guilt. Why did I get to have it so good when so many people were suffering? I didn't know how to express my many complicated feelings or to whom to express them. So I just held a lot of stuff in.

Luckily, there is a place in American high schools for misfits and weirdos with big, complicated feelings: theater club. On stage, I found a safe space to both explore my emotions and escape them. I made friends and worked really hard to lose my Croatian accent. As I learned how to disappear into characters, I also got better at blending into this new culture, and the teasing at school lightened up. And, fueled by a desire to take on bigger roles, my English comprehension improved rapidly.

When I was sixteen years old, just as I was finally settled into my new life in the United States, my former babysitter invited me to play piano at her wedding back in Croatia. I'm not a great pianist. I'd give myself a C− at best. There were other, more accomplished pianists she could have chosen, but we had really bonded when I was growing up and I think the spirit of the performance mattered more to her than my skill.

Going back to Croatia wasn't unusual for us, even with all of the war-related tensions. We visited every summer during my high school years. It's strange now to think that we kept returning even though parts of Croatia were occupied, forcing us to fly into Budapest, Hungary, and then drive the rest of the way home—four long hours crammed in a van with my family, news radio on full blast the entire ride, and no AC.

On the day of my former babysitter's wedding, the city suffered one of its worst attacks. I was certain the wedding would be called off and rescheduled, but the bride and groom decided to go through with their special day. They were sick of the war. Everyone was. They were tired of hate controlling their everyday lives, so they made the decision that fear was not going to win this time.

Instead of sitting in a basement that night, terrified, I found myself sitting in the beautiful, old church I had attended my entire childhood, in front of a shiny black piano, playing a very mediocre version of a gospel song. Despite, or perhaps because of, the chaos and violence outside, there was a lot of joy in the church.

After the ceremony, the wedding festivities continued with a reception in the basement cafeteria. Many guests hadn't made it to the wedding, including the best man, who was called up to report for duty and fight just that morning. Still, the party went on. The bakeries were closed, so some of the wedding guests prepared the food and desserts, and we dined on delicious homemade *sarma* and more varieties of cookies and cakes than I can name.

The windows of the building had long ago been blocked by sandbags, making the church basement as good a bomb shelter as any. I spent that night sleeping there with some of the other wedding guests, all of us lined up on the floor like sardines. What I remember most from that wedding isn't the grenades or fear, but the laughter and singing and the celebration of love.

What we didn't know at the time was that the day of my baby-sitter's wedding would mark the last major battle of the war. More than two hundred thousand Croatian soldiers fought along the four-hundred-mile front in what was the largest European land battle since World War II. Operation Storm began on August 4, 1995, and by 10:00 a.m. on August 5, Croatian soldiers raised the flag and declared victory.

As would any couple getting married, my former babysitter and her fiancé had a clear vision of what they wanted for their wedding. They put a lot of time and effort into planning it all out, wanting it to be just perfect. When war disrupted their fantasy, instead of giving up and canceling the festivities, instead of pining for what they wished could be, they accepted what was and made the absolute best of it.

I, too, have had specific plans. Plans for my life, my marriage, plans for the type of mother I would be. The way I dreamed it, I was going to get married and have a bunch of kids. Motherhood was going to fulfill me completely, and I'd be eternally grateful. My children would be well mannered and better listeners than all the brats I had babysat for a measly three to five dollars an hour. My children's father and I would have an ever-romantic, lifelong Romeo and Juliet type of love affair (minus the family drama and that whole death-pact part). We'd raise our children in a large, loving, stable home with well-trained dogs. And we'd all get at least nine hours of sleep each night. And we'd have a housekeeper. And maybe a live-in masseuse. And no stretch marks. Or chin hairs.

My postwar fantasies weren't disrupted by literal bombs, but there were certainly some figurative ones thrown my way. After surviving the bomb of my marriage falling apart while parenting two young kids, I dealt with stress bombs, barely-making-ends-meet bombs, the depression bomb, a weight-gain bomb, and the I-feel-worthless bomb. Bomb after bomb after bomb left me wondering if maybe, just maybe, everyone, including my children, would be happier and better off if I'd just disappear. For good.

I got so down on myself for not being able to provide my kids with everything that their friends' parents could. The children my kids had playdates with lived in bedrooms that looked as if Pottery Barn had vomited all over them. I'd hear other parents talk about planning vacations and family trips to amusement parks or signing up their kids for dance lessons, and I could barely contain my self-hatred. It all left me feeling like everyone else was living my fantasy, while my life spiraled out of control.

That year, I showed up to Luka's Halloween parade at school after a few hours spent beating myself up for throwing my kids' costumes together using whatever random things I could find around our house. Matea had really curly blond hair, so I took some old fuzzy white fabric, pinned it to her clothes because I didn't know how to sew, and said she was a sheep. I put Luka in a thrift-store vest and tie, and added a pin made of paper that said "#1 Teacher" to make sure everyone knew he wasn't just a kid in a worn-out fancy outfit.

I stood there alongside all of these parents whose kids were parading around in perfect store-bought costumes or elaborate homemade costumes, stewing in my own shame. But then Luka walked by, and I could see him searching the crowd of parents, looking at every face. And as soon as he saw me, his eyes lit up with joy and a huge smile spread across his little face. He wasn't searching the crowd for the perfect mom. He was searching for me, just me. Nothing more. Nothing better. Nothing different. Just me.

It is so easy to be negative when we're struggling. The list of things we don't have and can't do seems so much longer and more detailed than the very short list of things we do have and can do. My parents didn't have much when I was growing up, and I still had a wonderful childhood. My mom felt inadequate at times, and yet I remember so clearly being in third grade, trying to draw a picture of her in art class and just sitting there, staring at the blank paper because I didn't know how to draw her as magnificently as I saw her.

The most valuable thing we have to offer our kids isn't stuff; it's our love. I had to choose to stop focusing on the long list of things I didn't have and couldn't do, and instead focus on the things I did have and could do, no matter how small.

I spent one afternoon drawing and then cutting out big letters from colorful paper to create a banner for our bedroom that spelled out my kids' names. It was nowhere near the level of Pottery Barn decor, but my kids loved seeing large, colorful "Luka" and "Matea" on the wall, especially since those names aren't common in the United States. I started making picnics for my kids. I'd serve the same food we'd normally eat but add a twist to make our meals more interesting and fun for them. I'd cut peanut butter and jelly sandwiches into four or five odd shapes to create sandwich puzzles my kids would have to figure out how to put together, then pack our little lunch, grab a blanket, and walk my kids to the park. Those picnics created some of our best memories.

When Luka was almost four, he made it very clear that someday he wanted to be a mailman. Every time we would pass a mail truck, he would stare at it and say, "Ugh, I can't wait to grow up, just so I can finally be a mailman!" I was at the dollar store buying some snacks for his birthday party and worrying that our meager affair wouldn't compare to the other birthday parties he'd attended when I noticed a box of envelopes. An entire box for just a dollar. Inspired, I purchased two boxes.

My friend Jo had flown in all the way from the East Coast to spend some time with me. She had left her two young kids with her husband to spend five burning-hot August days in an apartment with no AC, sleeping on a mattress with the infant daughter she'd brought along, just to be there for me. The night before Luka's party, Jo and I stayed up late drawing stamps on each envelope and addressing them with funny street names. We strung the envelopes across the ceiling of my living room, and when Luka saw them the next morning, he was in awe.

A few days before the party, I stopped my mailman and asked him if he could possibly make an appearance at the party. I had even scheduled the party to coincide with the time when I knew he'd be out on his route and near our street. About an hour into the birthday party, there was a knock at the door. When Luka opened it and saw the mailman, he couldn't have been more excited. Our mailman not only showed up, he brought gifts from the post office—special envelopes and boxes my son could play with, an album for stamp collecting, and even a cool hat! I didn't have money to hire entertainment, but Luka appreciated the kind mailman's short visit more than he would have appreciated a clown or a magician. Focusing on my short list had come through for me again. It had also forced me to get creative and build my community in ways I wouldn't have if just throwing money at the party had been an option.

Parenting is insane. Even without any added financial burdens or depression, parenting is a circus. It's every extreme emotion all bottled up, shaken together like a strong cocktail, and then chugged by our brain cells. Parenthood is happy and sad, fulfilling and draining. It makes us feel like a superhero one second and a total failure the next. Parenting is complicated. Very, very complicated.

Choosing to embrace what *is* has saved me from feeling like I'm losing in life. I have to choose to embrace the unexpected and messy, to arm myself with a great sense of humor and a "good enough" attitude. When I don't have the perfect solution to a parenting dilemma, I have come to accept that winging it is an underrated but very respectable approach (to child rearing and piano playing and a whole load of other things). Winging it has always topped the short list of things I actually *can* do.

The fantasy I created for my life was always going to set me up for failure, even if I hadn't gotten divorced or struggled financially or emotionally. A fantasy is by its very nature unrealistic. When we create unrealistic expectations and fail to meet them, we feel guilty and inadequate. We're self-abusive freaks who need to lower our standards. When we take a moment to realize that perfection is an illusion, and we make space to accept our flawed, imperfect lives, we will find just how much power we actually have to make life wonderful. The best you can do almost always ends up being more than enough.

When I hit my lowest point, I thought I had to wait for this or that to happen before I could be happy. I was passively hoping someone would show up to give me tools and solutions, when all I needed to do was to start using the tools I already had. I falsely believed that if my circumstances would just change, my attitude toward everything would change, too. But it actually works the other way around. I had to stop pining for what I had imagined and make the best of what already existed. I had to stop chasing the fairy tale and start embracing the adventure.

I was standing in the way of my own happiness. The picnics, the mailman birthday party, my child's wider-than-a-jack-o'-lantern grin on Halloween . . . there were so many incredible moments of joy I would have missed out on, and, more importantly, my kids would have missed out on, if I had kept waiting for everything to be just as I once pictured it before I decided to fully live.

At that Croatian wedding years ago, it didn't matter that the bride and groom didn't have the dream wedding cake they had ordered or the perfect flower arrangements they'd envisioned. What mattered was that they showed up. They showed up, surrounded themselves with loved ones, and celebrated. And it didn't matter if my piano playing included some accidental notes. What mattered was that I showed up for people I cared about and embraced the joy that was right in front of me.

If we don't show up and embrace what is, regardless of how many unexpected bombs are thrown our way, we'll spend the rest of our lives waiting for something we'll never reach, when what is within reach is so, so wonderful. Imperfect and messy and chaotic, but wonderful.

Nine

Ne brini. Divno je.

My *baka* (Croatian for "grandma") and I were always close. From a very young age, I felt like she understood me. My hyper, animated personality could be too much for some adults. Not for her. I spent a lot of my childhood at her house in Serbia. I loved visiting her so much that every time I had to leave, I'd hold on to her, kissing her face, my eyes full of tears, thanking her for everything. She'd take my little hands into hers and say, "Don't cry. I'll see you again."

To get to my baka's house, we passed through a red metal gate and were then greeted by the perfume of the roses in her garden and the bright, sweet scent of strawberries and the sight of a gorgeous apricot tree.

My grandfather traveled occasionally, and when he did, I would get to sleep next to my baka in her bed. There was nothing better! I'd get all snuggled up in her big down comforter and ask her question after question. She'd indulge me and answer, saying, "Okay, but this is the last one I'm answering and then we have to get to sleep." Before she could object, though, I'd ask another one and she'd answer that one, too. I loved our late-night talks. She had this wonderful way of meeting me at my level but without ever patronizing me.

In the morning, I'd wake up to find her gone, and her side of the bed already neatly made, the white duvet with its tiny pastel floral print folded into tidy thirds and the matching square pillow fluffed. I'd rush to quickly make my side of the bed, but it never looked as neatly made as hers. I couldn't be bothered with making the bed perfect when I knew a perfectly great day was waiting for me. I'd run outside and see her in the garden watering the strawberries and tending to her roses. Sometimes she'd even talk to them, whispering to a wilting flower that any other person would have seen as hopeless, snipped off, and tossed. "You're still lovely," she'd say. My baka would look up from her garden, notice me still in my pajamas, and send me to get dressed for the busy day ahead.

Our busy days were all the same. We'd get on our bikes and ride to the market. (My grandmother didn't get her driver's license until she moved to the United States when she was in her seventies, after taking driver's ed in a foreign country with a bunch of sixteen-year-olds.) I'd follow my baka's bicycle over dirt roads into the center of town, while we sang silly songs at the top of our lungs the whole way. When we reached the downtown, we'd bump over cobblestones and trolley tracks and then arrive at the busy open-air market.

Once there, we'd talk about our cooking plans for the day and weave our way through the tables of fruit and vegetables looking for inspiration. The produce prices were sloppily written on pieces of torn cardboard propped against piles of fruit, as old women shouted out, "Try this! Try this!"

My favorite part of the market was the bakeries. It's no accident that carbs are my love language. Croatians are so passionate about bread that there are love songs in which the lyrics compare a lover's kiss to warm bread fresh out of the oven. In America you might say, "He's a great guy," but in Croatia we'll say, "He's good like bread." The market had a couple of little free-standing wooden shops where bakers sold gorgeous, oval-shaped loaves of bread that were crusty and golden on the outside and soft and white on the inside. The bread was freshly baked that same morning and we'd always buy two loaves—one for home and the other to rip up and eat warm on our way home, because it was too delicious to wait. Once we collected all the ingredients we needed that day, we'd put everything into the big basket on the front of Baka's bike and head back to her kitchen.

I wasn't one of those kids who merely liked helping my grandma cook for the sole purpose of getting my hands dirty or sneaking a few extra tastes of whatever she was making. Even at a very young age, I paid attention to every detail, as if she were revealing the secret behind a magic trick. When I was a toddler, I saw my grandmother make chicken by pounding the meat very thin, then dipping it in flour, then egg, then bread crumbs, and, finally, frying it in a pan. I spent hours outside searching for long, thin stones that looked like chicken cutlets, and then I dipped them in sand, then water, then sand again, and "fried" them in a puddle of water. Since as far back as I can remember, I would follow my baka around the kitchen and imitate everything she was doing. I was talkative, curious, loud, and always in her way. Yet she never got annoyed with me or told me I was too young to help. On the contrary, she encouraged and motivated me, praised my attempts, and allowed me to do some serious cooking when most people would've been scared to even let me near a stove. By the age of five, I was making tomato soup, and by twelve, I was making full meals—which my mother appreciated, because she never particularly enjoyed cooking (though she's really good at it!).

Baka could make even the most complicated dishes seem simple when she was in charge of the kitchen. I never saw that woman read a recipe or even use a measuring spoon. She somehow knew that a little of this and a little of that would make the meal exactly how she wanted it. My grandmother made everything from scratch. Growing up, I didn't even know that soup came in cans. I thought soup came after Baka got a dead chicken from a friend's farm and then plucked it in the front yard while I screamed at her from a distance in my most dramatic voice, "Tell me when you're done and it's all cleaned up! If I see a single feather, it will ruin my life forever and I'll never eat anything again!" She'd laugh at me while singing and plucking away.

As my baka and I cooked and baked in her little kitchen, she would tell me stories about her childhood. I soaked them up. Her childhood memories were much more interesting than any children's book I'd ever read. She told me about growing up in rural Croatia with seven siblings; an abusive, alcoholic father; and no money—not even enough to buy her a pair of shoes. As a child, she would wake up early every morning, while it was still pitch-dark outside, help around the house, then take the cows out to pasture and bring them back before finally getting ready for school. She had to quit school after fourth grade to stay home and help her parents with the cows and with taking care of her younger siblings. Sometimes I think the reason she had such a tolerance for my exuberance was because through me she was able to experience the carefree, playful childhood she never really had.

As a young teenager, she was forced to leave home and move to a nearby city to live with a wealthy family and work as their servant, while sending her earnings back to her parents. One Christmas, the family she worked for told her they no longer needed help and that her employment was over. She headed back home, but her father rejected her. He didn't want to worry about another mouth to feed. So back to the city she went, looking for another family to serve.

Baka was a warrior. I found out at a young age that she was also a worrier. From as early as I can remember, my baka would tell me, "Kristina, you and I are so much alike. We both love to make up silly songs. We both love climbing trees and getting messy. We both love cooking. We both love people and showing them how much we care by creating things for them. You got all those traits from me and I'm glad you did. Those are all good things. But you also got something I wish you hadn't. You worry. You worry too much. I've spent my entire life worrying. I don't want the same for you."

As I grew older, she told me more about her life, about marrying my grandpa, who had lived through his own set of challenges, having survived being in a Communist concentration camp after World War II. She shared with me the hardships they faced as they started their life together and struggled to make ends meet. She endured many trials, but none compared to losing four of her six children. Her twin girls died within a day of being born; they were premature and there were no incubators available at the time. Her last baby died during a traumatic childbirth, a birth that almost took my grandmother's life, too. But the hardest loss of all was Daniel's death. Daniel was her second child, a boy just a year younger than my mom. Through tears my grandmother told me the story of his sweet little voice, only five years old, begging her one evening, "Mom, can I please sleep next to you in your bed tonight?"

"No, sweetheart, you're a big boy. You need to sleep in your own bed."

The following day, Daniel died in a tragic vehicle accident. It was the greatest pain of my baka's life. "Kristina, if I had just known. . . . If I had just somehow known that I'd never get to hold him again, I would have allowed him to sleep next to me that night, wrapped up in my arms."

I don't know how a person survives losing four children, but she did. She would say that her faith in God got her through, days and nights spent on her knees praying and sobbing and begging for comfort. She doubted a lot of things in life, but she never doubted God, and that faith gave her solace that someday she'd see Daniel and her three girls again.

My grandmother believed in the power of prayer. She not only started and ended each day with prayer; she prayed all day long. Whether she was cooking or gardening or expertly sewing a dress that I had sloppily designed on a piece of paper, in her mind she was constantly engaged in ongoing conversations with God.

She'd also sing old hymns as she went about her day. "'When peace, like a river, attendeth my way, / When sorrows like sea billows roll; / Whatever my lot, Thou hast taught me to say, / It is well, it is well with my soul!'" That particular hymn, she'd tell me, was written by Horatio Spafford, who had lost his young son to an illness, and only a few years later lost his four daughters in a shipwreck. He wrote the song in his greatest moments of grief, searching for peace, the same peace my grandmother so desperately wanted to feel. She would sigh and then reiterate, "Don't be like me. Don't spend your life worrying. Worry is the opposite of peace. My worry has never fixed a single problem. It didn't add anything to my life, but it took so much away."

With all that my grandmother had endured, it's not surprising that she was a worrier. She knew what it felt like to have life surprise you in the cruelest ways, and it's almost as if she were always preparing herself for the next strike.

As the years passed, my grandmother's life got easier, more comfortable, and less complicated. When my family moved to the United States during the war in Croatia, my grandparents came along and moved in with us. My grandmother had so many people in her life who loved her, admired her, respected her, and some who even envied her. And yet the worry never left.

When I became an adult, she'd occasionally ask me to trim her hair. She was much happier with me doing it than going to a salon, despite the fact that I had no training. She would sit patiently, telling and retelling me stories I'd already heard dozens of times. I never minded hearing them again. There was always something new for me to hear in them. I'd finish her haircut, full of disclaimers, warning her that it was far from perfect and that

I really didn't know what I was doing. But she'd just take my hand, kiss it, and say, *"Ne brini! Divno je!"* Which in Croatian means, "Don't worry! It's wonderful!" She was wonderful. She was always wonderful to me.

Toward the end of her life, my baka had many health issues. Eventually, she couldn't read because her eyes were in so much pain. She may have had only a fourth-grade education, but my baka had such a deep love of learning. She taught herself English, mainly by reading, and she particularly enjoyed history. I walked into her bedroom so many times to find her with her nose buried in a biography of one American president or another. But for the last few years of her life, she could no longer read or take the long walks she once enjoyed daily. When I'd call her on her birthday she'd say, "Oh, Kristina, I was really hoping not to be here for this birthday! I'm ready to go."

The very last day I spent with her, we sang together once again. I sat beside her bed in the nursing home she'd settled into after moving back to Croatia, and we sang "Amazing Grace" in Croatian. She reminded me once more that we were so alike, and she urged me not to waste my life worrying.

As I was saying goodbye to her, tears streamed down my face. I knew full well that, unlike all of our other goodbyes, this one would be final. I hugged her and held on to her, just like I did after each visit with her as a child. I kissed her face, my tears smearing onto her cheeks, thanking her for everything—for how much she loved and believed in me. She took my hands into hers, which were beautifully wrinkled and shaky, and said, "Don't cry. I'll see you again." And then she leaned in and whispered, "Where the roses never die and where there are no more goodbyes."

And no more worries either, I thought to myself. *No more worries.*

The morning my mother called to tell me that my grand-mother had passed, I felt such sadness, and yet such joy. Never before had I felt those two emotions so strongly at the same time. My baka was ready to go; she had been praying that God would take her. I was heartbroken that I couldn't just pick up the phone and hear her voice once again, yet I was also overjoyed that her worries were over. My baka's name is Mira (pronounced *Mee-ra*), a name derived from the Croatian word for "peace" (*mir*). She was finally at peace.

I couldn't sleep the night after she died. I kept thinking about her life. I thought about the way she treated everything living, from people to her garden, with such hope. She worried about her own life, but the moment someone else was struggling, she was there to encourage them and not let them dwell on their fears.

Like her, I worry about everything. In my late teens and early twenties, I ended up with ulcers from all my worrying. Despite my hard-won certainty that worry never fixes or solves anything, both my grandmother and I kept worry around, kind of like an old friend you know is destructive but who has been your friend since childhood, so it's hard to part ways. Because what's familiar, even if it's unhealthy, becomes comfortable.

Having children only amplified my worrying. I don't think there's been a day in my life as a mother that I haven't worried. I worry about big stuff and small stuff and everything in between. There's a saying in Croatian, *"Ne daj Bože djetetu što mama misli,"* which basically means "God, don't let a mother's thoughts actu-ally happen to the child." Because our thoughts suck. They just suck! Mom brains anticipate the worst. When our teenager is half an hour late, we think, *What if he's stuck somewhere and can't get help? What if he got into a horrible accident? What if . . . What if . . . What if . . . ?*

Those what-ifs have fully moved in and made themselves very much at home in my mind. One day, as I was worrying to my friend Amy, giving my fears way more attention than they deserved, Amy interrupted me midsentence and asked, "But what if the opposite of that ends up being true? Of all the things you've ever worried about, how many of them actually ended in a catastrophic tragedy? Didn't it turn out that with most of those worries, the opposite actually happened? Why are you creating a problem that doesn't even exist yet? And when the best possible outcome happens, you won't be ready at all to dig in and start living your best life. You'll only be prepared for the bad stuff to drop into your lap!"

Amy was right. I am always getting ahead of things, jumping to conclusions, and creating new problems instead of just waiting to address problems if and when they actually arrive. And if there is only a 50 percent chance that what I worry about might happen, then there is also a 50 percent chance the opposite might happen, so why do I always choose to give the negative outcome all of my time and energy?

On the rare occasions when the stuff I've worried about actually ended up coming true, all my worrying ahead of time did nothing to help. When I was broke, did worrying get food on my family's table? Nope. When I thought I was miscarrying, did my worry help that pregnancy thrive? Nope. But we trick ourselves into thinking our worry is protective or preventative, that working through every possible scenario somehow prepares us for the worst. But our negativity does not immunize us against the fall-out or stress of the worst-case scenarios when they arrive. We live in this pretend horrible world, just so that we might avoid being surprised if something terrible happens, which so often leads us to missing out on all of the good stuff that is right in front of us.

My constant worrying also means that I unintentionally fall into the trap of parenting out of fear. It's easy to get caught in that with young kids, but it's even easier to fall victim to when parenting teenagers. The scary parts of parenting aren't optional. That's a fact. But constantly worrying about our kids' futures won't change their futures, though it will make us miserable in the present.

For years, I used to dread the Fourth of July. Here's what it looked like from my perspective: I'd spend the day cooking whatever red, white, and blue side dish I signed up to bring, show up at friend's backyard party, and pretend I'm totally into this day. Then the fireworks would start and I'd freak out. But only on the inside. On the outside, I'd act like a totally normal, carefree human enjoying this happy, happy day. I'd kindly excuse myself from the backyard, faking a headache, and quietly slip inside the house until the fireworks were over. See, anyone who has experienced war will tell you that fireworks, unsurprisingly, sound exactly like other, less festive kinds of explosions. No matter how many years have passed since the last time I heard actual grenades as a child during the war in Croatia, as soon as the fireworks show starts on the Fourth of July, I tense up. Fireworks give me anxiety, a feeling of uneasiness, an urge to run to the nearest basement. What is in my head is powerful.

Then, a few years ago, it finally hit me: instead of hiding inside, I need to look at what is actually in front of me. If I *see* the fireworks, maybe I can disconnect the sounds from the war and be present for what is really happening. And you know what? It works! Now when I hear fireworks starting, instead of running away from them, I run toward them. I immediately go outside, looking for them, so that I can see them for what they truly are. When we live inside the what-ifs and our memories of every bad thing that has happened in our past or every bad thing that could happen in the future, we miss the possibilities for joy and beauty. Though there is a lot we parents can worry about, if we're willing to get out of our little dread-filled cocoon and keep our eyes wide open, we'll find there's actually more to celebrate than there is to fear.

There is one more complication to parenting from a place of fear: our children learn from watching how we live. What am I teaching my kids about fear when I let it have so much power in my life? Our kids sense our fear; they see our clenched jaws and sweat and will pick up on and mirror whatever energy we project. With my teenager Luka, in particular, I have often found myself approaching him to have a conversation consumed with worry before either of us has even opened our mouth. The negative, stressful tone this sets for our conversation is not only unfair to my child but also keeps me from enjoying motherhood. With fear leading the way, even the most ordinary interactions feel tense, heavy, and doomed.

My first step when I wrangle my persistent worry is to recognize that I won't be able to just pray my fears away, the way my

grandmother tried to do. There are things in life we can completely overcome and there are things we have to learn to live
with, without letting them get the better of us. I have had to accept fear as part of my DNA, but I do not have to allow it to run
the show. Taking control of my worry means first noticing when
I'm worrying and then recognizing that worry is a feeling I'm
experiencing and not objective reality. Learning how to be aware
that worry is just a feeling has helped. What also helps is looking
back at all the times I worried and was gripped by my fears and
still chose to just walk through it. You know those bold, thrill-
ing moments that make you feel alive and suddenly give everything meaning? Yeah, those moments don't happen when fear is
in charge.

Here's what I've been working on lately: What if I choose to
replace worry with hope? Not passive, head-in-the-clouds, fluff-
type hope but real, active hope. Hope that is equipped with infor-
mation, bolstered by common sense, and fueled by love. Hope
that doesn't allow negativity and fear to lead me. Hope that isn't
just a thirty-day trial with a great return policy but, instead, a
lifetime commitment. Hope that is confident in the fact that I will
do what I can for my family, for myself, for our future, and when
I notice that I am worrying, I will choose to imagine not the
worst-case scenario but the equally probable best-case scenario.
And I will keep pushing forward, believing that in the end we
will all be okay.

On successful days, I find myself walking toward my teenage
son to have a serious conversation about something worrisome
and the moment I feel that familiar anxiety fill my chest, I turn

right around and walk away. *Nope, you're not approaching this conversation with fear, Kristina,* I tell myself. Then I take a deep breath and think about how my grandmother would have wanted me to talk to my child. With hope. The same hope she always gave me. The same hope she gave even a wilting rose.

Ten

Recovering Pessimist

When my firstborn turned six months old, I decided that this milestone was definitely worth celebrating. And what started as a one-off event quickly became a family tradition: For my kids' half birthdays I make half a cake (it looks like someone just cut a cake down the middle and made the other half disappear), and we sing every other syllable of the "Happy Birthday" song (I'm really good at complicating things, and singing only the first half of the song seemed unfair to the second half). We don't do gifts or a big bash, and we don't blow out candles and make wishes, because wishes should be made only full throttle. We just end the day with a little celebration after dinner, something kind of silly and fun. And cake. Because everything in life should end with sugar.

This little tradition brought so much joy to our family that I decided we should celebrate other random days, too. I wanted to make more of an effort to celebrate successes (big or small) but also to celebrate the not-so-fun-but-just-as-important moments in life. When a friend of ours lost his job because the company he worked for was downsizing, I asked him if we could throw him a party. With his enthusiastic consent, I sent out an Evite invitation for an "I Got Laid Off Party" to celebrate our friend's new beginnings. If anyone else had ever been laid off, we would celebrate them, too. Getting fired usually means that you sit on your couch feeling crappy and panicking about the future alone. But how much nicer is it to deal with disappointment when you're surrounded by friends who share stories about the times they were fired? And also cake. Obviously.

About a year after Ari was born, Philip and I decided that he should have a vasectomy and that if his balls were going to endure a painful procedure, they deserved a party. We sent out invites to our close friends that featured a photo of a lemon with the caption "All juice, no seeds!" I prepared a menu of meatballs, spicy cheese balls, Cuban stuffed-potato balls, Sicilian arancini (risotto balls), cake pops, truffles, coconut almond balls . . . well, you get the idea. Balls. Only balls. Earlier that year the New England Patriots were accused of deliberately deflating footballs before the Super Bowl in what became known as the famous "Deflategate," so I bought a bunch of little footballs from a party store, let out the air, and those became the party favors: deflated balls. So two days after Philip's vasectomy, as he sat on the sofa with a bag of frozen peas on his crotch, our house was filled with our favorite people and a lot of laughter.

Why all this fanfare and fuss for the little stuff? Well, the truth is that I don't naturally see the bright side of things. My default worldview is pessimistic. (Probably in part because I'm

Croatian. I don't know if you've ever delved into Eastern European literature, but let me tell you, it's pretty bleak stuff. Brilliant! But bleak.) I consider myself a recovering pessimist. I have learned to go out of my way to proactively create my bliss. Finding the good in life is a struggle for me and a conscious choice I have to make daily, since, apparently, you can't have Amazon Prime just deliver a box of happy to your house. They sell pretty much everything except for the stuff I really need: joy, patience, naps.

I noticed early on in motherhood that my children inherited my tendency toward the negative. Years ago, while driving home from a soccer game, I was listening to my kids whine about their day. Practically everything made their list of complaints, and I was sick of it. I decided something had to change, so I made up a new game.

"All right, Luka and Matea," I yelled from the front seat, "I have a new game for us. It's called Yeah, But. Every time you have something negative to say, you have to follow it up with a 'Yeah, but . . . ' and then add something positive. I'll start. Ugh, I'm almost out of gas and the last thing I feel like doing right now is stopping at a gas station. Yeah, but . . . I have a car! And I have money for gas, and I don't ever want to take those things for granted. Okay, your turn now."

Luka quickly spoke up. "We lost our soccer game, and I'm really upset about it. Yeah, but . . . I love my team and my coach, and I'm glad we have another game next week."

Then Matea chimed in. "I was really bored today all day. Yeah, but . . . tomorrow I have a playdate with Siena!"

The Yeah, But game has become a regular exercise in our

home. I don't allow my kids to dwell on the negative. They can complain, of course; I welcome them to express their aggravations and concerns and I think it's really important to let them talk through those feelings. But then I try to encourage them to find something positive in whatever situation they're dealing with. There are too many good things in their lives (in all of our lives) to let the days fly by without pausing to acknowledge our blessings, and I would be doing my children a disservice if I allowed them to always just wallow in the negative.

To compare the pitfalls of focusing on the negatives to food (since eating is my favorite sport), brooding over the annoyances, disappointments, frustrations, failures, pain, and resentment is like marinating chicken. A few hours or even a full day is good. But if I let that chicken sit in the marinade for weeks or months or years . . . instead of ending up with a dish that I can proudly serve to my family, I will end up with a gelatinous poison. Same protocol applies to negative feelings. We should allow ourselves to feel what we feel. Take a dip in that marinade. Let the marinade make us more tender. Get a little seasoning. But don't leave yourself marinating forever. The Yeah, But game is a way to finish the marinating process before it gets out of hand.

That night during the war in Croatia when the shrapnel from the grenade flew through my bedroom window, it hit and destroyed the bookshelf that was right behind the head of my bed. The entire thing collapsed onto my bed and shattered into pieces. (Another reason I'm thankful that I wasn't sleeping in my bed that night.) The thing on that shelf that meant the most to me was a photo album my mom had put together. Pretty much every photo she had of me, from birth to twelve years old, was in that album and it was almost completely burned. We had no digital backups or negatives, so we had no way of reprinting those precious memories. There are about ten pictures of me as a child that I rescued from the little corner of the photo album that was still intact. Most of them had charred edges.

When I was thirteen, I was so angry that my childhood photos had been destroyed that I took a pair of scissors and cut off some of those charred edges. I guess it was my unsuccessful way of trying to erase any reminders of what had happened to my photos. During my senior year of high school, a teacher asked us to bring in a kindergarten or first-grade photo of ourselves for a project. I didn't have a photo of myself at those ages. And I didn't feel like explaining why, so I just didn't do the project. I pretended I forgot about it and accepted an F on the assignment.

Later on, in my adulthood, I was complaining to my mom about how much it bothered me that I didn't have many childhood photos. "I don't even know what I looked like at certain ages. It makes me really sad." My mom listened and let me take a dip in the disappointment marinade, and then she said, "I understand it's really upsetting. And of course you're sad about it. But also keep in mind that that's the only meaningful material possession you lost in the war. Your photo album. You have friends who lost everything."

She was right.

She didn't point this out to suggest there was something wrong with me for feeling sad about the album; she was just reminding me that I needed to put my loss in perspective and realize how much I had to be grateful for. Yeah, but . . . how amazing is it that at least that one corner of the album didn't get burned?

Yeah, but . . . my parents' entire home could have been destroyed and it's still standing to this day. Yeah, but . . . I could have been in my room that night, sleeping in my bed, and then I might not even be here to be sad about the photos I lost.

I want to make sure I'm clear on something here: I'm not in any way suggesting that we should suppress our feelings or our pain because someone else has it worse. I've been on the receiving end of comments like "Well, you don't have it as bad as so-and-so, and you need to get over it!" Or "Your being upset about that one event is an insult to people who experience it daily!" Or "I went through that, too, and it didn't affect me the way you're saying it affected you, so you must be lying or exaggerating your pain."

Whether it was about my divorce or my depression or even something as sensitive as being sexually assaulted both as a child and as an adult, I've received feedback that has made me feel like my feelings aren't valid. I can tell you from experience: those words aren't helpful and they don't lead the recipients to gratitude or happiness. Statements like those come from a place of judgment, and judgment has never helped anyone become a more positive person.

We have a right to feel what we feel! Suppressing our feelings or being shamed for how an experience is affecting us is not the path to healing. Each individual experiences things differently. We are not weaker for processing things in a different way than someone else might, and we are not liars or "too dramatic" for feeling something more deeply than someone else. We need to acknowledge, respect, and fully experience our own emotions, even the "bad" ones. But once we've taken whatever lessons those negative feelings have to offer, we have to get ourselves up out of the marinade, grab a towel, and start actively looking for the good that's around us, even when it seems impossible to find.

My mom was diagnosed with a rare form of cancer a few years back. The diagnosis was a complete shock because there is no cancer in our family history. None. She underwent a full hysterectomy and has been doing well since. About a year after her surgery, she flew from Croatia to visit me. On one of our morning walks through my neighborhood, I said, "I feel bad that you're spending so much of your time here just cleaning up after the kids and cooking for all of us. I want you to enjoy yourself!"

"I am enjoying myself! I enjoy every moment," she replied.

"There's no way you enjoy cleaning, Mom. No one enjoys cleaning."

"Kristina, I didn't think I'd be here today. I didn't think I'd ever see my grandchildren or you again. So, yes, I enjoy cleaning. I enjoy every moment I get."

Her words hit me hard. Why does it take something as big as a cancer diagnosis to get us to appreciate every single moment we have on this earth, to find the pleasure even in the mundane?

When I drop my kids off at school in the morning, I often frame my farewells with an emphasis on their responsibility to look for the good. Instead of saying, "Have a great day!" I'll say, "Choose to make it a great day!" Because I do believe it is a choice. We've all met people who seem to have it all and yet are completely miserable. And then we've met people who have next to nothing, have weathered many trials, and lost so much, yet carry themselves with such lightness. There's a Croatian saying that goes *"Svako je kovač svoje sreće."* It means "Everyone is a blacksmith of their joy." We should make an effort to create happiness in our lives instead of blaming our unhappiness on everyone and everything else.

I suck at a lot of things. (This isn't me being a pessimist; this is me just being a realist.) Toward the top of that list would be keeping New Year's resolutions. Or any resolutions. Frankly, I find resolutions kind of aggressive and intrusive, like they're just staring at me with judgment, waiting for me to fail. Every time I've tried setting resolutions, I've ended up telling them to go pound sand. But one year, I decided to try a different type of New Year's resolution, one that seemed a little friendlier.

I decided that every single evening for an entire year I would write down something good that had happened that day. Not something general that I was thankful for, like my family or friends or great weather. I knew that in order for this activity to be effective, I needed to find something very specific that happened on each particular day. Easier said than done, but so is getting out of bed in the morning or making breakfast or driving a car or any of the other thousands of things we mindlessly accomplish on a daily basis.

During that year of searching out one great thing every day, I applied for a job I really wanted. I felt like I was a great fit for the position, but I didn't get it. Under normal circumstances, I would have allowed the bad news to ruin my entire day (more honestly, I would have milked it for months!) and I would've gone to bed solely focused on this negative experience. But with this new resolution as my priority, I had to think of something good that happened that day—something that I probably would have overlooked otherwise. After some thought, I wrote down that the grilled Nutella and goat cheese sandwich I had for lunch was lovely and orgasmic. (I know that combination might sound bizarre, but if you have any self-love, you'll try it.)

That same year, I found out I was pregnant for the third time. The decision to try to conceive a child was one we'd thought through, and after just two months of trying, Philip and I were ecstatic when that second pink line showed up on the pregnancy test. The timing was perfect! If you're married to a CPA, you're not allowed to deliver a baby in March, April, September, or October, so we were aiming for a pretty narrow window of time before we'd have to press the pause button on our fertility plans. But we'd nailed it! Our baby would be due in December, just days from when Philip's parents had already planned a trip to visit for Christmas. I made my children T-shirts that said "Big Sister" and "Big Brother AGAIN!" and we videotaped their reactions as they unwrapped the shirts and realized that, after years of begging, they were finally going to have a little sibling. They kept hugging and kissing my stomach. Matea cried with excitement and asked me cute questions, like "Mommy, can I teach the baby how to roller-skate?" My heart was so full.

In our third month of pregnancy, my husband surprised me with a romantic trip to San Francisco for my birthday weekend. The night of my birthday, Philip had made reservations at a nice restaurant. I was excited to get my glam on. I slipped into a really cute midi dress; it was white and strapless and flared out below a fitted bodice, with a sweet pink ribbon that tied around the waist. I felt like Jackie Onassis. We were about to head out the door when I decided I should probably pee quickly before we left, because, you know, pregnancy. So I went to the bathroom and sat down. And then I saw blood. My heart dropped.

I'd spotted a little for one day when I was pregnant with Matea, but this was different. We called the midwife, called the doctor, and went to urgent care in San Francisco, but it was the weekend and we couldn't get any clear answers from anyone. When we returned home two days later, I went in for an ultrasound and, to our surprise, found out that I was carrying twins. One of them hadn't made it. Everyone seemed to agree that this was the cause of the bleeding.

So many powerful and opposing emotions hit me at the same time that I almost felt drunk. Ever since my grandmother had told me the story of her twin girls who were born premature and didn't survive, I'd dreamed of having twins. Finding out that this dream had actually been a possibility but was now gone filled me with such a deep sadness. And then I thought, *Yeah, but . . . the bleeding I was so worried about means we lost one, but we still have another. We're still having a baby.*

Within two days, though, we found out that the other baby was in trouble. For the next week and a half, I had more doctors' appointments, ultrasounds, and blood tests than I could count. Every day I seemed to be getting different news. One day we found out that, unfortunately, there was a very small chance this baby would actually make it. But then a day later everything looked hopeful. And then it didn't again. And then it did. Only a handful of people knew we were pregnant, but I remember not wanting anybody to ask me how it was going. *Don't force me to give you a clear answer when I don't have any clear answers!* I thought. I pinballed between despair and hope and guilt and excitement and fear and relief and sadness and emotions I don't even know how to name.

About two weeks after I first saw blood in San Francisco, Philip and I went back to our doctor's office for yet another visit. They'd taken some tests the day before, and when I checked in with the receptionist, the nurse asked if I'd seen my lab results. "They're really good!" she said, sounding quite cheerful. Suddenly I felt more hopeful than ever, giddy, even, about the pregnancy. I snuggled up next to Philip in the waiting room and started chatting about the cute little onesies on display in the clinic's boutique. When the nurse called my name, I practically skipped down the hall into the ultrasound room. I lay down on the examination table, Philip standing next to me, both of us anxious and excited and hopeful. But it wasn't long into the ultrasound when I saw the look on my doctor's face— the look of someone who knows there is no good way to say what has to be said. Our baby had no heartbeat.

In moments like these, it's a wonder that your body continues to fill your lungs with air when you've forgotten how to breathe.

The doctor gently informed us that I needed to have a D&C procedure to remove everything from my uterus, and she gave me the options of being transferred to the hospital, where I'd be put under full anesthesia, or staying at the clinic, where I'd have to be awake during the procedure. I thought about the long drive to the hospital, and the paperwork, and having to sit in another waiting room for hours with this grief and dread, and I couldn't face it. If this nightmare was really happening, I wanted it to be over as quickly as possible. I elected to stay at the clinic.

"Are you sure?" the doctor asked. "I can numb you a bit, but it's a very painful procedure." I didn't care.

"Do what you need to do. I just want to go home."

I sat there while they gave me shots and pills to prepare me for the procedure, and I couldn't stop crying. I kept thinking about how angry I was, how I couldn't believe this was happening to me. I couldn't imagine that I'd have to go home and break my kids' sweet little hearts with this news. Philip and I felt like we were already starting to bond with this child. My daughter had put her mouth right up to my belly button and promised to share her room and her toys. I had gotten myself excited and invested in a future that wouldn't exist. We all had so many hopes and dreams for this baby. And now those hopes and dreams were gone. I couldn't wrap my mind around the idea that within an hour, my pregnancy would be officially over. Just like that. Over.

The procedure was excruciatingly painful and traumatic. I felt violated even though I knew this had to happen and everyone involved was only trying to help me. The doctor and nurse kept handing each other strange tools and using medical terms that I didn't understand. Because it was a surgical procedure that required a sterile environment, Philip wasn't allowed to be in the room with me. I lay there and tried to be brave, but the pain was so intense and kept getting worse.

"Just breathe, sweetie. You're doing great. We're almost done," the doctor kept saying.

I was in so much physical and emotional anguish that I couldn't take in any comfort. I wanted to scream at her, "How could you possibly know what I'm going through? Have you had this done?!" But maybe she had.

Tears were streaming down my face and I was grabbing on to the bed as tightly as I could. And then suddenly, instead of focusing on the pain, I chose to start focusing my negative thoughts on something else.

We wanted another child so much. Yeah, but . . . I'm so thankful I have Luka and Matea.

I can't believe I won't get to hold these babies. Yeah, but . . . my sweet husband is waiting for me right outside the door, and he can't wait to hold me.

This hurts like hell. Yeah, but . . . time will make the pain more bearable.

I feel so empty right now. Yeah, but . . . the blessings in my life have always and will always outnumber the losses.

That night, back at home, I lay in bed staring at the list I had kept of all the good things that happened each day that year. I was supposed to write something down for today, but I wanted to skip the exercise just this once. The day had been a nightmare. Telling my older children had been as devastating as I'd predicted: Luka was shocked and angry. Matea was completely inconsolable. I was emotionally drained and I was still bleeding because of the D&C. There was nothing good to report. Nothing! But I had promised myself that I would write down something good, something specific, every single day. After a few hours, I was finally able to find one specific good thing to write down: the way Philip had so sweetly tucked me into bed after bringing me home from the clinic.

I know that sounds really simple and maybe even insignificant to some, but if I hadn't committed to finding good in each day, I would have fallen asleep that night consumed with negativity, with how much I hated everything about that day. Instead, the last thought I had before I fell asleep was: *I am loved. I am so loved.*

Eleven

Control Freak

When the midwife handed me my first baby, I felt like such a badass. Just a few hours earlier, I'd been pitifully saying my goodbyes and telling my mom and husband to take good care of the baby because the grapefruit I'd been mentally preparing to push out of my vagina felt more like a giant brick wedged horizontally in my pelvis and I was convinced I was going to die. But then my son Luka popped out, and in a flood of emotions and hormones, I felt myself transformed from a woman who looked like roadkill into Beyoncé strutting onstage in a fierce outfit, or Katharine Hepburn sitting down fabulously and instructing the nearest man to give her a cigarette. I was in complete control . . . for about seven solid minutes. And then my Luka peed all over my bare chest.

Apparently, I could not control his bladder.

Then he started crying, and not only did I not know how to calm him, I didn't even know what he was crying about. Then he made his own decisions about when he would and would not sleep, which of course never matched up with the "sleep schedule" I'd carefully prepared. I tried every lullaby I knew, in English and in Croatian. I tried everything in every baby book I'd read and put into action all the advice—solicited and unsolicited—anyone gave me. But he never slept until he decided he was ready to.

And then he refused to eat as much as I needed him to. He started losing weight and we had to go to a lactation specialist, which is where you sit on a couch while strangers whip out your boobs and wiggle them into your child's mouth. I don't think anyone has ever given my breasts as much attention as those two lactation specialists (who I remember only by the nicknames I gave them: Titty Fairy and Nipple Navigator). But Luka still wouldn't nurse. Eventually they filled a syringe with milk I'd pumped, connected it to some thin plastic tubing, taped the other end of the tube so it ended right next to my nipple, squirted the milk directly into Luka's mouth to get him excited, and then slowly moved the tube away until my son was actually sucking on my nipple.

For weeks, I repeated this laborious procedure at home every two hours. Many nights I cried. My baby and I both lived completely covered in milk. (If your kid prefers the bottle to the breast, you do *not* need to put yourself through this. Your kid will be fine. But Luka was as uninterested in nursing from a fake nipple as he was in engaging with a real one, and I figured if I was going to have to teach him how to suck on something, it might as well be my breasts, because they were easier to carry around when we went out.) I'd always imagined that my child emerging from my body and latching on to nurse would be this beautiful, effortless bonding experience for us. Instead I was taping tubes to my boobs and squirting milk with a syringe, sometimes accidentally straight into Luka's eyeballs, just to try to get my kid to gain a little weight so he wouldn't have to be hospitalized.

Soon after becoming a mom, I heard a song called "If I Could" by Celine Dion. As I listened to the lyrics, staring at my sweet baby's face, both my love for him and my fear for him felt more real than ever. I sobbed. The lyrics were torturous, I tell you, especially for someone still struggling through the crazy emotions of postpartum blues:

> *If I could*
> *I'd protect you from the sadness in your eyes*
> *Give you courage in a world of compromise*
> *Yes, I would*
>
> *If I could*
> *I would teach you all the things I've never learned*
> *And I'd help you cross the bridges that I've burned*
> *Yes, I would*
>
> *If I could*
> *I would try to shield your innocence from time*
> *But the part of life I gave you isn't mine*
> *I've watched you grow*
> *So I could let you go*

. . .

If I could
I would help you make it through the hungry years
But I know that I can never cry your tears
But I would
If I could . . .

As tears streamed down my face, I wondered how I could ever be at peace loving someone with every molecule of my being and yet knowing that I would never be able to shield him from the inevitable sadness and pain life would bring his way.

Within the first few months of Luka's life, I learned to let go of a lot of the little things I'd thought would be within my purview as his mother. But as Luka got older, the smaller, simpler things that I learned to accept were out of my control became bigger, scarier things that were out of my control. As his world expanded, I found myself craving more and more control, and yet found my control diminishing. It was terrifying.

I want to control everything. I always have. But once I became a mom, my desire for control became an urgent need for control. Control seemed like my only weapon against a world that promised to hurt the thing I loved most fiercely, one way or another, some day or another. Any parent who says she has zero control issues is either a liar or a liar. However, I knew that if I wanted to avoid emotionally suffocating my children and to feel even semi-successful as a mom, I would need to let go most of the time. But how was I supposed to know how much to let go and when?

Could I keep control in my life as, like, a friend? Demote it from the "I want to be all over you every waking and sleeping moment because I can't live without you" zone to the friend zone? Or would I have to completely unfriend control?

As our children grow from babies to walking toddlers to driving teenagers to on-their-own adults, we're supposed to let go a little at a time, right? Or maybe a lot at a time? How much and when? Why hasn't someone written out the exact formula for this? Or discovered medication that induces letting go (preferably with side effects that include patience and a constant state of feeling rested)? The longer I've clocked in for this motherhood gig, the more I've learned and failed, then succeeded and failed again, at letting go.

One area in which I learned to control my controlling tendencies was with the things that didn't matter in the long run. When Luka had to create a solar system in third grade, my imagination immediately went into overdrive, brainstorming how we (and by "we," I meant "I") could make his version of the solar system unique and spectacular.

"What if we figure out a way to make it out of glow-in-the-dark balloons?"

"No, Mom."

"Okay, what if we make a little movie where we have different people act out each planet? And then you can show the movie in your class. That's genius! I can't believe I just thought of that!"

"No, Mom."

"All right, all right . . . I have something even better! We love to make fun cakes, right? So what if we made a solar system–shaped cake? Each planet could be a completely different flavor, and we'll use fondant to create cool, elaborate details. And then your class would get to eat the cake afterward. Yes! Yes, we're doing that!"

"No, Mom. I just really want to make it out of Styrofoam balls like the example the teacher showed us in class."

Oh, you mean the overdone boring version that EVERY SINGLE KID in your class will make, I said on the inside. "Sure, that sounds great!" I said on the outside, faking an excited expression so hard that my jaw was sore for days.

I knew my response to Luka's assignment was all about my ego. Who cared how creative he got with a third-grade assignment? The outcome didn't matter as much to Luka's growth as the process of completing a big assignment as independently as possible. I was going to have to land the parenting helicopter and let Luka do it his way. If I butted in, I would send him the message that he couldn't handle projects on his own, that he wasn't creative enough, or that his ideas were not as good as mine. I had to let go and allow him to do his own thing . . . as I stood in the background—cringing but still pushing encouragement through clenched teeth. "Well, that's . . . that's . . . different . . . and so awesome!"

And he'd look over at me, big smile on his face, feeling confident. "Yeah, it *is* awesome."

Two years later, when it was Matea's turn to create a solar system, it turned out she'd been eavesdropping on my conversation with Luka and she remembered all the suggestions I'd had for him. She excitedly told me that she'd like her solar system to be made out of cake. I was ecstatic! I immediately emailed her teacher, getting permission to bring a homemade cake to school to share with her classmates, and then started designing the cake in my mind. I had a *vision* for this cake. Every planet was going to be a different flavor, we were going to use lots of marzipan and fondant to add shape and color, and somehow I was going to figure out a way to make the planets look like they were actually floating. It was going to be epic.

But then Matea told me her idea for the cake. What she envisioned turned out to be little half globes covered in messy frosting representing the different planets, perched on a superthin, lopsided sheet cake. "This is so great!" I forced myself to say. And truly it was. With no fondant, no elaborate details, and with only one flavor and a million imperfections that I refrained from fixing, the solar system cake was great. Because it was *her* vision that *she'd* realized. If I'm being completely honest, it was hard to ignore the petulant disappointment I felt at first. Hey, I'm human. But after I stepped away from my own ego and my desire for control, I was able to joyfully appreciate that my independent daughter had taken notice of a great suggestion, carried it in her mind for two years, and then confidently executed her version of my suggestion when the time came.

Over the years, I also learned to let go of my expectations when it came to things like teaching my kids how to make their beds. When they were young, my kids would complete the chore of making their beds, and I'm sure they did their best, yet it invariably looked like, you know, a little kid had tried to make the bed. I'd see one corner of the comforter folded over weirdly and part of the sheet hanging out, and my first urge was to go in there and fix it. (I'm not even a clean freak, it was that disheveled!) But then I'd pause and ask myself a question I've found really helpful in motherhood, one I've learned from older parents who have been there and done that: *Will this really matter in the long run?* No. No one ever died from living in a home with poorly made beds. I've googled it. What matters is that I empower my kids and avoid sending them the message that the way they do things isn't good enough. So I told them their beds looked great and let it go. Kristina: 2; Urge to Control: 89,768,201. But who's counting?

When Luka and Matea were starting sixth and fourth grade, we moved to a new town. We were all very excited. It was the first time we could afford to buy a home, and we were moving from a small apartment to a house with a backyard (my son's wish) and stairs (my daughter's wish). Philip and I were thrilled to have more space, in a town with a great school system, and in a neighborhood full of kids.

But I could also feel myself stressing out about my kids starting a new school. Luka had struggled at his previous school; he'd been picked on and hadn't really developed strong friendships. It broke my heart to listen to stories of him getting turned away or shut down by other kids. Luka handled it as well as a kid can, but still, I know it hurt. I wanted so badly to have some control over how he would experience his new school, to set him up so that he never felt alone or rejected. I wished I had the power to get ahead of him and fix everything, including things that weren't even broken yet.

A few days before their first day at school, I found out that Cat, my only friend in this new town, lived in a house that looked out over the school's playground. Well, how convenient! As they got dressed for their first day, I slyly convinced my kids to wear bright yellow shirts so they would be easy to spot. Cat's kids knew the bell schedule and when the students would be outside for recess. Just before 10:50 a.m., I showed up at her house with binoculars and headed for her bedroom.

I heard the distant sound of the school bell and watched nervously as the kids started to fill the yard. I'm not completely sure if what I was doing was legal, but I'm completely sure it was unacceptable: a middle-aged woman pressing binoculars against a window, staring through them, and tracking the movements of innocent schoolchildren.

With a thrill, I spotted the neon-yellow shirt my son was wearing. But Luka was standing all by himself, not a single kid around him! I wanted to cry. I saw Matea in the distance, playing with two girls. She seemed to have already made friends. My eyes returned to Luka. He was standing near the basketball court. Other children were already on the court, casually dividing up into teams and starting to play while Luka just stood by and watched. I wanted so badly to jump out of that window, run across Cat's yard, leap over the school fence, and tell those kids, "See this kid here standing on the sidelines? He's really nice! Play with him! He's a really cool kid. I'll give you twenty dollars each, just give him a chance!" It's moments like these when I'm grateful I don't get to enact in real time every parenting idea that crosses my mind.

After a few minutes, a boy started walking toward my son. As I watched, I began to cheer out loud. The only other time in my life that I ever felt so invested as a spectator was when Croatia played France in the 2018 World Cup Final. And that time, I literally peed my pants. "Come on! Keep going! Keep going, kid! Keep walking toward him!! Ten more steps! You got this!!!" (Thankfully the window was closed and soundproof—otherwise, I'd be writing this from prison. And my son might never have spoken to me again.) Just as the kid got close enough to Luka that I was convinced he was about to start a conversation, he abruptly bent down to grab something that had been sitting on the grass near where Luka stood. The kid picked up the object he'd been looking for, turned around, and walked away, seemingly without even noticing that Luka had been there at all. "NOOOOO!!! What are you doing?? You're walking in the wrong direction, kid! Go back!!!"

My inability to control this situation was killing me. I wanted to fix it! I wanted to make it better for Luka. I wanted my son to be noticed and accepted. Why couldn't I just stage-manage this interaction?

Finally, after what felt like an eternity but was probably just a few minutes, another student carrying a basketball approached Luka. I started jumping up and down. "Come on! Come on, man. Take a few more steps. I believe in you! Don't turn around. Just keep walking toward my boy!" Then, boom! The kid said something to my son. And then my son said something back. I froze, taking in every tiny movement and gesture. The kid handed the basketball to my son . . . and they started playing together! Tears streamed down my face. We won! We won this one.

I put the binoculars down and unglued my body from the window. I felt like I had just completed an emotional marathon, and though I was exhausted (like, actual sweat running down my chest), I realized that not being able to control everything gave me an opportunity to witness something I really needed to see: my boy, out there in the big, scary, sometimes mean world, standing strong by himself, staying open, and then making a friend.

It took my kids a few weeks to adjust to their new school and develop friendships, but soon enough, they were both telling me how happy they were that we moved. And I was able to fully retire my binoculars.

A few months later, news of another devastating terrorist attack took over the internet, newspapers, and television. Soon after that, yet another school shooting occurred. A friend of mine called me asking for advice on explaining the unexplainable to her children. The latest tragic headline news had occurred in a town neighboring hers, and there was no way to shield her elementary school–age children from it. "They're so young, Kristina. They shouldn't even know this kind of hate exists in the world. I'm so pissed off that I don't have the ability to control what my kids hear about or what they see. Or what they fear." I recognized that desire to control what passes from the world into our kids' minds and hearts. And I wished I had some brilliant, rock-solid advice in my back pocket that could give her and all parents a sense of total security. After crying with her for a while on the phone, I suddenly had a realization. "I think we just have to empower our kids, give them something positive to do, something good that they actually can control. The worst thing a kid who is scared can feel is powerless and hopeless." It's probably no coincidence that the worst things a parent struggling with control issues can feel are exactly the same: powerless and hopeless.

When we hung up, I sat down and started writing a letter to my children, and to her children, and to all children who are introduced to the ugliest parts of humanity at such a young age.

What I didn't realize at the time is that I was also writing it to myself.

To my children, and all children, after yet another terrorist attack:

I wish I could fix it. I wish I could fix the broken, hurting parts of this world you are growing up in. I wish I could shield you from the hatred and sadness and fear that we sometimes see. I wish I could tell you that it's all just a bad dream and the whole entire world is perfectly perfect and peaceful, and that nothing terrible like this will ever happen again. Ever.

But I can't. I can't fix it. I can't get rid of all the pain in this world. And I can't even give you all the answers, because sometimes there are no answers to this type of hate.

But there is something I can do. And more important, there is something that you can do. When really, really bad things happen, it's hard not to feel helpless and weak and scared. But I'm not helpless, and neither are you. We have a very important strength, and that strength is called "good."

It may sound simple, and it is. Often the most powerful things are the simple ones.

Think of the world as a big bucket. Some people try to fill the bucket with hate. They try to hurt people, they try to bring fear and sadness. It's so shocking and sad that sometimes the good guys just stand there overwhelmed, feeling helpless, and they lose sight of the power they have. And if good guys just ignore the bucket while those wanting to bring pain keep filling it, the bucket will be filled with bad.

Here's the great news: there are way more people wanting to do good in this world than people who are wanting to add pain. Most people in this world are good. So if the good people, like you, start filling the bucket with good, the bucket will have more good than bad in it, and eventually it will overflow with goodness and love and kindness.

Every good person can add good to the bucket in their own way. Adding good can mean being a friend to someone who is lonely. Adding good can mean giving away a toy to someone who needs it more than you do. Adding good can mean baking cookies for a soldier or firefighter, or taking blankets and food to the homeless. Adding good can be drawing a beautiful picture for someone who isn't feeling well, or cheering up someone who is sad with a sweet, funny note.

There are thousands of ways to add good to the bucket, and none of them is too small or insignificant. So when you feel scared or when someone tries to add hatred to the bucket, use your special strength and keep pouring more and more good in.

Every little drop of good matters. You matter. You are not helpless. You are the good this world so desperately needs.

Control can easily become obsession, and our obsession can tighten around us like a chain, preventing us from having range of motion—and emotion—to live a full life.

Similarly, I have a hard time letting go of negative emotions just because they are negative. Negativity itself isn't motivation enough to get moving; I need something healthier to actually walk toward. Instead of just stifling the energy I give to my controlling tendencies, I have to channel those impulses and redirect that energy. I need to do something positive. I need to add good to the bucket.

As a parent, I've learned to make my plans in pencil, not Sharpie. Two Christmases ago was our first holiday season in a new house and I was eager to make some new memories with my family. My ex-husband was sleeping over, as has become a tradition on Christmas Eve, so that my older kids can have both their parents on Christmas morning. The tree was decorated, the presents were finally wrapped, and I had stayed up late, prepping both Nutella and cinnamon buns so all I'd have to do in the morning was take them out of the fridge and pop them in the oven. Just as I was finally ready to crawl into bed at 1:30 a.m., utterly exhausted yet completely excited for the following morning—a mix of feelings many moms I know associate with Christmas Eve—I heard my son Luka screaming in pain. I ran to his room and found him burning up with a fever and clutching the lower side of his stomach, just above his hip. I woke up his dad, who was in the guest room, and we rushed to the emergency room together. After a CAT scan, we were told he immediately needed surgery to remove his appendix.

So instead of spending Christmas morning surrounded by my whole family, eating homemade cinnamon buns in my pajamas in my new home, I found myself once again, just like the day Luka was born, in a hospital with my firstborn and his dad, being reminded of how little in this life I can actually control. I watched on FaceTime as Ari and Matea and Philip opened presents while my ex-husband and I sat in our teenager's hospital room, eating vending machine food. My amazing son cracked jokes through his pain and we made plans to hold a memorial service for his appendix, which Luka had brilliantly named "Jimi Appendrix." On the television set in the background, Forrest Gump sat on a bench telling a stranger, "My momma always said, 'Life was like a box of chocolates. You never know what you're gonna get.'" Yup, Forrest, I know exactly what you mean.

Twelve

Mind Your Own Motherhood

On the flight to meet Philip's parents, Lou and Judy, for the first time, I informed Philip that sometime during our weeklong visit, I'd like to have a frank conversation with his mom about my relationship with her son. I was planning on waiting until we'd had a few days to get to know each other, and Philip agreed that waiting was a good idea.

But apparently, I'm not good at waiting (especially when it comes to waiting to talk). So on the same day we arrived, only a few hours after meeting Philip's parents, we were out for dinner when I turned to Judy and said, "I want to talk to you about something important."

Philip gave me his surprised "Really? Already?" look.

Philip is much more patient and rational than I am. He usually tries to get through the introductory small talk before delving into deep and serious soul-searching. I don't know if it's my blunt Croatian culture pushing through or something more individual and innate, but I'm allergic to small talk and I couldn't resist the impulse to cut straight to the real talk and lay everything out on the table.

I dove right in. "Judy, I want to talk to you mom to mom, and I want to be completely blunt and honest with you. If my son comes to me one day and tells me that he's met a girl he's in love with, that she's divorced, that she's the single mom of two very young kids, that she's barely making it financially and has dealt with a lot of depression and stress in the past few years, I would have some major, major concerns, to say the least. And to be honest, that type of girl would probably not be my ideal dream for my son, not exactly what I would hope for him. So, if you have any concerns about me, about your son dating me, I completely understand. I get it! And if you have any questions for me, I want to be as open with you as possible, so please know that there is absolutely nothing you can ask me or say to me that would be out of line."

Philip's mom looked at me and, echoing the same passion and sincerity with which I had just spoken, responded, "And I want *you* to know that I have never seen my son this happy. I have had many honest conversations with him since the two of you started dating, and I have no concerns. And I also want you to know that if someday you marry my son, and I hope you do, those kids of yours will be my grandchildren, and I will treat them as such and love them just as much as I love my own blood."

I was relieved. And I was also shocked. Her response was not what I had expected. This woman had an incredible ability to let go of any expectations she might have had for her son and his potential future spouse and to embrace me for who I was, flaws and all. It would have been so easy for her to decide that she didn't like me and that I wasn't good enough for Philip before even meeting me. But instead she decided to give me a chance. She decided to trust her son's judgment and to get to know me for who I really am—my full story, my heart, and my intentions.

Over the years, my friends and viewers have shared horror stories about mothers-in-law who have dealt out harsh criticisms, shamed them, or excluded them. But women receive a lot of judgment from another source, too, one without family ties but one that can do just as much harm. I'm talking about the judgment that comes from fellow moms, the ones we run into at school pickup, the ones we work with, and especially the ones we interact with on social media.

Mom shaming seems to have become an accidental hobby for some people, and most moms have been on the receiving end of a heaping dose of judgment from another parent at some point. I've been criticized for being a stay-at-home mom and criticized for being a mom who works outside the home. I've been criticized for being too strict and for being too lenient. I've been criticized for breastfeeding in public. (Which, I mean, come on! The only time public breastfeeding should bother anyone is if an adult stranger walks up to a woman, latches on to her breast, and then starts nursing. Without permission. That should definitely bother people. Other than that, there is really nothing to see, people. Move along.) I've had fellow moms roll their eyes at me for making homemade bread for my kids. (As if I were trying to prove my womanhood. Nope. I just like homemade bread. Carb addict. Can't help it.) I've had moms roll their eyes at me for feeding my kids chips and salsa for dinner. (It. Was. A. Rough. Day.) My own mom raised me the same way, able to cook from scratch some days and slapping together something quick and easy on other days. Sure, I could use some therapy. But not for that!

On a flight back from visiting family in Croatia one summer when Ari was two years old, he screamed bloody murder for hours. Hours! Here's something no one warned me about before I was a mom: parents who are flying with young children don't rest on flights. (Also, vacationing with your kids isn't an actual vacation. It's the same old exhausting motherhood routine but with a prettier view.) Ari couldn't fall asleep earlier in the day for his usual nap, so by the time we were seven hours into our eleven-hour flight, he was completely exhausted and delirious.

I was carrying him up and down the aisles, trying to soothe him, but my precious, precious, precious little boy (if you say "precious" enough times, your child will seem precious even when there's nothing precious about him #liesitellmyself) wasn't just screaming with his vocal cords, he was screaming with his entire body, arching his back and thrashing like a little porpoise baby. I struggled just to keep him in my arms. Everyone was staring at us. Some people looked concerned. Some people looked annoyed. Some people looked like they wanted to murder us. My child was *that* child, the child you never, ever want to be stuck with for a long flight in an enclosed capsule in the sky.

I, somehow, very awkwardly, while pretending I still had a touch of gracefulness left in me, managed to get myself and the precious maniac I was holding to the back of the airplane without his taking anyone out with his "passionate" acrobatic moves. I folded myself into the restroom with him to give the other passengers some peace, but I could stand to be stuck in that tiny little box that smells like urine with a screaming child for only so long before I completely started to lose my marbles. I left the restroom and crouched down in the back of the plane, holding him while he continued kicking and punching. I was singing to him, I was bribing him, I was trying to breathe slowly so he wouldn't sense my stress, and then in the middle of all this chaos, a woman approached me with a very annoyed look and asked me, "Um, ma'am, did you forget to feed him today? Because he's obviously hungry."

Was she serious? Had I fed him? No. I didn't think to feed him today. I feed my children only on special occasions. Then a few minutes later (a time span that felt like weeks of excruciating torture), another person approached me and in a very harsh, preachy tone said, "You need to put him down. He doesn't want to be held. Put him down!"

WE WERE ON AN AIRPLANE!!! If I put the kid down, he would throw himself through the aisles and hit a beverage cart. Or he would cause immeasurable chaos, screaming in other people's faces, punching and kicking *them*, and we would be asked to leave the airplane immediately, which, by the way, would really suck because we were flying over the Atlantic Ocean at that moment. (And speaking of beverage carts, what I could have really used was a beverage or three or five, but nobody was offering me one. I was offered only judgmental looks and advice. Brilliant, useless, unsolicited advice.)

And then, a little while later, with my son still screaming as if he were trying to make sure all the passengers in all the other airplanes in the sky heard him, too, yet another person approached me. This time, there was no judgment on his face, no hatred shooting like lasers out of his eyes. The man looked at me in the most caring way and said, "You're doing great. I just wanted you to know that. I know how you feel. I've been there, flying with my baby years ago. Hang in there. You're really doing great." My shoulders instantly relaxed. With a few simple sentences, that man relieved me of so much stress. With tears in my eyes, I wanted to scream, "You win!!! Ding, ding, ding, ding, ding!! You win, sir! You are the winner of the compassionate, decent human award!!"

Eventually, my toddler exhausted himself into oblivion and slept. But I can tell you with 100 percent certainty that it wasn't because I followed the advice of two strangers who assumed they knew my child's personality, medical history, feeding schedule, or family dynamic better than I do.

When someone shames a well-intended parent for their choices (and, yes, this includes a mother-in-law rolling her eyes at the fact that her daughter-in-law runs her home in her own way), the shamer is declaring that they know everything there is to know about every possible life and parenting scenario. Shaming indulges an incredibly arrogant impulse. I think in some cases, the root of this arrogance is really insecurity.

Truth is, there isn't *one* correct way to parent, so if someone's way of parenting is different from yours, they aren't doing it wrong . . . and neither are you. Different doesn't equal wrong. You don't have to agree with other people's choices. No one is forcing you to. The only time we should spend any energy focusing on how someone else is choosing to parent (or live) is when we want to learn something from them. Otherwise, mind your own motherhood.

I'm going to be honest with you. I used to be the type of person who believed that every thought and opinion I have should come out of my mouth. I used to believe that giving voice to everything I felt made me an honest human, a blunt and bold and brave human. What I didn't take into account back then was that before we can hear hard truths, we have to feel loved and safe and accepted. Without that security, we won't get past our feelings of rejection or pain to consider the content of the (perhaps loving) criticism.

If my good friend Cat sits me down and tells me I might want to rethink how I'm handling one of my kids, I can listen to her and pay attention and not feel for one second like I'm being mom-shamed or bullied. But that's only because I *know* her. I know the purity of her intention. I know that she is on my team. I know her heart and that it is as full of love for me as mine is for her. Trusting relationships take years and a lot of energy to build, and it's worth investing that time and energy because you'll end up with a friend whose truth you're able to hear. Always. And that's one of the many gifts a true friendship can give: with the right history, even the hardest feedback can land the right way.

It took years of being on the receiving end of criticism from people I didn't feel safe with for me to figure this out, but it also took becoming a parent. So often we're told to treat others the way we'd want to be treated. But most of us are so freaking mean to ourselves! Becoming a parent gave me an easy way into this perspective: I try to treat people the way I want people to treat my kids.

I really let it fly in one of my videos and indulged in a rant about what a complicated day I'd had with my kids. I was sure there was another mom out there who needed to hear that her kids aren't the only ones who misbehave and that her family is normal. That evening, once my kids were tucked in bed and finally asleep, after checking on them seventeen times (because that's normal, right?), I hopped online to peruse the comments my dear audience had left for me. One woman's feedback stood out in particular. She wrote, "What is wrong with you and all these other mothers agreeing with you? My children are all grown now and I can tell you that they NEVER behaved in a disrespectful way or broke my rules because I raised them right!" I rolled my eyes and shrugged it off. By that point I had gotten used to at least one stranger each day lecturing me on how unless my children are perfect, I suck as a mom.

Later that same day, I received a private message from another woman, in which she explained that the judgmental woman who hadn't been willing to get off her high horse and had to brag about her perfect children on my page was . . . this woman's mother. And you'll never guess what. This woman was a bit of a rebel when she was growing up. And she claimed her siblings weren't perfect every second of the day either. But their mom either didn't notice or was in denial—in deeply, because the most important thing in their family was having perfect children who would reflect perfectly on her. As adults, this woman and her siblings weren't as close to their mother as they wanted to be. But none of them was keen to confront her about their flaws—or her own.

That judgmental, snarky comment under my video clearly came from that woman's own insecurities, her own pain. Those who judge and shame others (and disguise it as "I have a right to share my opinion") are often the most insecure and miserable people. Think about it. Have you ever met a super judgmental person who was actually genuinely happy and fulfilled? Nope. Insecurities and dissatisfaction with one's own life lead to judgment; judgment leads to unkindness; and unkindness leads to even more insecurities. And so it goes, round and round, only adding hurt to everyone involved. It's important to note that most judgmental mom shamers don't actually see themselves as judgmental mom shamers. They just like to share their opinions. Out loud. So here's a really easy, single-question quiz to figure out if you're an ass or not: Does every opinion you have need to be voiced? If your answer is yes, you're an ass.

I've been asked over the years how I handle my haters. The answer is: I don't handle them. Because they're not mine to handle. When someone is judging you, it's unlikely that their judgment is actually about you. As I see it, we're all carrying around a bunch of suitcases. We have our insecurities suitcase. We have our stress suitcase. We have our guilt and our worries suitcases. Some suitcases we might have been carrying since our childhood, stories we were told about who we are that aren't even true. They're fiction that we were handed, picked up, believed, and still carry. Sometimes a person comes along with one of their suitcases, with their issues all packed up and ready to go, and they try to hand it to us. Do not pick up that suitcase! Do not pick it up! Because if you pick up their suitcase, you will be up all night, worrying if what they said about you is true, stressing yourself out, questioning yourself, getting bitter, and feeding your insecurities. Over a suitcase that never even belonged to you in the first place.

So if people keep trying to hand off their suitcases to you like you're a bellhop, you might need to break up with them the same way you would break off an unhealthy relationship with an emotionally abusive boyfriend. And as you go through life, trying to figure out how to ferry around those suitcases that do belong to you (and we all have our own stuff . . . the stuffiest of stuffs!), don't try to hand those off to someone else as a way to try to get rid of your pain. Instead, sit down with a friend or a great therapist and have a big, nonjudgmental "let's unpack these suitcases together" session.

As for those people in your life with whom you don't have the option of breaking up, but who insist on throwing unsolicited suggestions your way, just find a stock answer and then make it your auto reply: "That's interesting. I'll give that some thought." Only it's not, and you won't. You're making them feel heard and dodging a back-and-forth discussion that will only leave you feeling judged or pissed off. Life is hard. You are never going to please everyone with your choices, so put your kids' needs and your own sanity before other people's opinions. Stop taking on other people's expectations. They're suffocating. Those expectations are like a straitjacket and they will drive you insane.

We have a choice, daily, as we're interacting with people, to add good or to add hurt. And isn't there enough hurt in the world? I mean, seriously, there is so much pain in the world already. On any given day, you can check your social media and see a story of another suicide or another child being abused in some unimaginable way or innocent people being mistreated or killed, halfway across the world or in your own town. Personal pain is not a game of dodgeball, though. You can't take your ball of pain, chuck it at someone else, and then be free of it. Being a crappy human will only increase your pain, not heal it.

Parenting is so freaking hard! It's harder than anyone warned us it would be. So when our fellow parents—human beings like us who are raising children, who have kids looking up to them—choose to put hurt into the world by making horrible, mean comments whether in person or by hiding behind their screens on social media, the cut feels especially deep. So much of how we exercise our insecurities and fears comes down to competing and comparing, and no parent should ever feel like raising children is a competition. If you like to compete, great! Join a soccer team! Pick up tennis. Friendship and parenting are not competitive sports. (By the way, here's a big, fat secret I discovered to finding more joy in motherhood: stop comparing and competing. That's it. Seriously. Try it.)

The shaming I see and hear about every single day (not exaggerating . . . thanks, internet) has made me extra grateful for my mother-in-law and her nonjudgmental approach to our relationship and relationships in general. Years after that frank conversation we had when we met for the first time, we were sitting at a happy hour, sipping our cocktails and eating our favorite meal: bread with a side of bread. Judy told me a story about an evening out with a bunch of ladies her age. One of them mentioned that her son was dating a girl and that it was getting very serious. All the ladies chimed in, asking, "Well, what do you think? Do you like the girl? Do you like her?!?" My mother-in-law quickly spoke up and asked, "More importantly, does she like *you*?!" Everyone immediately shut up. Apparently, no one had thought of it that way before.

Judy doesn't treat me as her inferior. She doesn't make me feel like I should be pining for her approval. She doesn't try to call the shots in my life. She consults me when it comes to making decisions that involve my children and she doesn't expect me to do everything exactly the way she does. I'm sure she doesn't necessarily agree with every choice I make, but she lovingly holds her tongue and gives me the space to figure this gig out myself. In other words, she minds her own motherhood. Judy has shown me through the way she's treated me that it's not a woman's place to offer another woman unsolicited advice about her marriage or parenting or home. Ever. Even when that woman is her daughter-in-law. And because of those healthy boundaries, I actually like going to her for advice and asking for her input. Having Judy in my life has made me really think about the type of relationship I want to have with my future kids-in-law. I don't want to screw it up! I really, really don't. The mother-in-law/daughter-in-law relationship, especially, has had a nasty reputation for centuries as being one of the most volatile known to mankind. It's such a complex relationship with high stakes. Both parties come saddled with expectations and, in many situations, treat their relationship as a competition of who will be the stronger influence on the husband/son. And considering I'm not into competing with other humans, I definitely don't plan on competing with my future daughter-in-law. She comes first in my son's life. I don't. That's just the way it is once my kids are grown and married, and if my pride ever ends up having a problem with that, well, it's just gonna have to learn to suck it up.

Now, just to be completely honest here, I'm very well aware of the fact that I'm an impulsive, hyper person who gets extremely excited when I have an easy solution to a problem, so I may find myself accidentally blurting out a suggestion to my kids-in-law with the intention of simply being helpful. And while it will be my job to be aware of these tendencies and rein them way in, I'm hoping that I will have built the type of relationship with my kids' spouses where they trust that I'm never coming from a place of judgment. And that's the bottom line, isn't it? None of us wants to feel judged for doing what we feel is best for our family. And, hopefully, if we are decent human beings who work hard at not allowing our insecurities to turn us into asses, we do our best not to be the ones dishing out judgments and shame. Everyone deserves an open and honest attempt from others to let them be who they are and to live and parent the way they deem best. (Hey, future kid-in-law, if you happen to read this . . . just know that it would make me absolutely giddy to think I'm able to make life a tiny bit easier for you with my advice. Solicited advice, of course. Only if you ask. Please ask. Also, while I have your attention, I want you to know that your loving my child will be the greatest gift you will ever give me, and there's nothing more I'll ever need from you. Except maybe a few grandkids. But only if you want. Please want. Okay, I'm done.)

Whether it comes to in-laws or friends or complete strangers, being a jerk is a voluntary condition. It's not genetic. We actually have a choice. We just have to stop ourselves before sharing our opinions or advice and ask, *Could this potentially add unnecessary hurt? Am I the right person to say this to this person? Is now the right time to say this? Would I want someone to say this to me? Am I arrogantly behaving like my way is the only right way?* And if something potentially painful absolutely HAS to be said, ask yourself, *How would I want this to be said to me?* Or better still, *How would I want this to be said to my child?*

Let's say you're on a plane next to a woman whose baby just can't seem to stop crying. And you genuinely want to be helpful and really, truly, deeply believe that that child desperately needs to be held. There's a big difference between telling that mother, "Your baby needs to be held," and saying something like, "If it's okay with you, do you want me to hold the baby for a few minutes so you can take a nap? I've totally been there and know how exhausting traveling with young children can be."

If you're at all uncertain of your ability to stick the landing on a delicate, sensitive social interaction like this, all you need to say is, "You're doing a great job." And then you can use the earplugs you brought with you because you knew you were going to be in a metal tube in the sky for several hours and that other people would be flying in that tube with you because they need to get somewhere, too, and some of those people might have children, and sometimes children cry. Kind of like when you go outside and it might be windy, you bring a jacket. Be prepared. It's always a good idea to pack some patience and empathy, because you were a baby once, too; keep that in your pocket. And when you find yourself starting to focus on the negative in others? Just ask yourself, "WWJD? What would Judy do?"

Thirteen

The N-Word

When Luka was seven, our conversations as I'd walk him to school would often get pretty deep. On one such morning, the subject of self-control and the power of the words we choose dominated our walk. As we crossed the street, I caught a glimpse of Luka's face, bright red and as pinched as a few years back when he'd had to admit that, yes, he was the one who'd filled the toilet bowl with toy race cars. He looked . . . guilty. He's never been able to keep things from me for too long. He has to get his worries off his chest, even when he isn't sure how I'll react.

As we reached the far curb and stepped up onto the sidewalk again, Luka took a deep breath and then blurted out, "Mom, I try really hard. I do. But sometimes I say things I know I shouldn't."

"What kind of things do you say, Luka?"

"Well . . . don't be mad at me, but . . . sometimes I say the N-word."

My heart stopped.

"Luka. Luka. Luka." I was trying desperately to stay calm and to keep the shock I was feeling from exiting my mouth in the form of a raging scream. "Luka. When? When do you say that word? Why? To whom?"

"Sometimes I just call people that. At my school. Other kids. I just go up to them and say, 'You're a . . . ' and then I say the N-word. And then I kind of laugh. And then run away."

I started sweating. I felt like I couldn't breathe. The town we lived in at the time was very diverse. In fact, Luka and Matea, with their pale skin and blond hair, were in the minority at their school. I loved that because I believe that raising children where they are surrounded by many different races and cultures sets them up to be more open-minded, more understanding, and less judg-mental. Ever since they were really young, I have talked openly to my children about racism and bigotry in general. What did I miss? How did my child, *my* child, think using the N-word was okay?

"Luka, why? Why would you use that word?"

"It's just funny, Mom."

My voice was shaking and thick with emotion. "It's not funny at all! Have your teachers heard this? Have you gotten in trouble?"

"Yes. Don't be mad, Mom. But I did, I got in trouble for it. They told me to stop. But then I did it again."

How had I not gotten a phone call about this? I could never show my face at the school again. And those kids! Were they going home in tears, telling their parents about this little white boy who kept calling them the N-word?

As my son and I reached the school, I crouched down to his level and grabbed both of his hands. "Look at me. Look at me and listen to me very carefully. You are not allowed to use that word.

Ever. That word has a really sad story behind it that I will explain to you after school, and that word hurts people." My eyes started to fill with tears. "There is already so much hurt in this world, buddy. We should never do anything to add more hurt. We should only add kindness. Okay?"

"But, Mom . . ."

"No, Luka. No buts right now. Just promise me you will not use that word!"

"But, Mom, it's not a big deal! You're making it a big deal!"

Deep breath. Deep breath. Deep breath. NOT A BIG DEAL?!? Had the sweat pouring out of every humiliated and horrified pore of my body not given him a hint that, yes, this was a big freaking deal?

And then Luka, this child I had treasured and studied and adored since the moment he was born, looked at me with the sweetest, most innocent face. "But, Mom, it's just a body part—nipple."

Nipple. The N-word was "nipple." He was calling kids a nipple.

My heart started beating again, my breathing returned to normal, and I no longer felt the need to move halfway across the world, where no one knew me. Turns out, I wasn't raising a racist. I was raising a weirdo. What I assumed would be a mountain turned out to be just . . . a nipple.

Luka's sharp wit and deep thinking has always made him both a joy and a pain in the butt to raise. I love him to pieces and have learned that often the children who challenge us the most also teach us the most. Because the more curveballs we're thrown, the more capable we become at handling anything that comes our way.

One particular afternoon when he was almost eleven years old, a day no different from any other, I was sitting in the living room working on my computer when Luka walked in and announced, "We need to talk." He looked serious, even a bit nervous. I figured something had happened at school that day. Maybe he got picked on or got in trouble for talking too much.

He continued, "You need to put your computer away and really listen because this is important."

I started to get a little worried. My boy usually expressed his thoughts quickly and spontaneously, even the ones that mattered the most to him. This was different. This was big.

"Mom, I realized something and I thought you should be the first to know. And after we talk, I'd like to call Daddy and tell him."

He sat down next to me on the couch, seeming older and more mature than ever.

"Okay, buddy. What is it?"

Luka took a deep breath and said, "I am ready to come out of the closet." Another deep breath. "I am straight."

I sat there frozen for a second, staring at him. My first instinct was to laugh at how cute this was, but my stronger instinct was to pause and reflect on what had just taken place in our living room. This wasn't a joke to my son. My boy was being completely genuine and he needed me to take him seriously.

In Luka's mind, his important announcement made complete sense. He knew that when people are gay, they often "come out of the closet," and they usually disclose their identity first to the people closest to them. He figured that "rule" applied to everyone, because we are all human and should play by the same rules, straight or gay. When you've figured out that part of yourself and are ready, you share it. You come out.

I gave him a big hug and told him how honored I was that he told me first. And then I looked at him with tears in my eyes and told him that I would love him straight or gay, because that's not what makes someone lovable or not. What makes someone lovable is their heart and their actions. And then I thanked him for opening my eyes to the type of world I want to live in.

I want to live in a world where gay children don't have to feel like outsiders, don't have to play by different rules, and don't have to prepare a big coming-out speech or be terrified of whether or not their mom or dad will love and embrace them for who they are. I want to live in a world where everyone comes out. Everyone. Gay and straight. A world where parents wouldn't assume anything. We wouldn't suspect or gossip. We would wait. We would listen. We would believe our kids when they tell us who they are. And then we'd let them know that they are wonderful and they are loved just the way they are. I want that for others because it's also what I want for myself—to be accepted for who I am. Isn't that what we all want?

And I also want to live in a world where people don't use words to hurt people, don't use words as weapons in general. A world in which parents realize how important it is to teach acceptance and kindness—more important than making sure our children wear matching socks or that they finish that last bite of asparagus or get perfect grades. And it starts with us. It starts in our homes. Are we modeling for our children how we should treat people, both in person and on the internet? Do they hear us gossip and mock people? Are we teaching our children that being different isn't a bad thing? Are we showing our children that disagreeing with someone doesn't give us the right to be unkind?

Are we putting too much pressure on our children? Do our children know that they are really, really loved even when they mess up? Are we teaching our kids to stand up for people? Are they seeing us stand up for people? Are we providing a peaceful home so that our children feel they have a safe place to fall? Are we creating an environment in which they know they can come to us with the uncomfortable stuff and the embarrassing stuff and the scary stuff and the stuffiest of stuffs, and we won't shut them down? That we will listen?

Words are more powerful than we think they are. And the master class in equality Luka gave me that afternoon was far from the last major life lesson he'd teach me.

A few years back, I had one of those lucky days where I'd been awake for only two hours, yet had already accomplished 763 days' worth of work but somehow had nothing to show for it. In other words . . . motherhood. The morning was stressful. Everybody was running late, one of the dogs peed in the kitchen, the other threw up on the carpet, the littlest kid was cranky from teething, the oldest one couldn't find his shoes, and the middle one was taking forever to eat her breakfast because apparently my hysteria wasn't a good enough indication that I needed everyone to hurry up, get their crap together, and get in the freakin' car. The fact that I wasn't ready either was obviously beside the point. My stress needed a target and my kids fit the bill.

Once everyone was finally in the car, I gave a long, loud lecture to my older kids about being ready on time and responsible for their own belongings. I thought it was a pretty solid lecture. I'd give it at least a B+. Lots of anecdotes, peppered with some profound thoughts—maybe even some quotable stuff—and delivered with great passion (and by "passion," I mean anger, but "passion" makes me sound like a lovelier person so I'm going with that).

I finished my brilliant speech and Luka, who was twelve at the time and not the silent type, sat in silence. Finally, I asked, "What are you thinking?"

"Nothing. You wouldn't understand."

"Try me."

He spoke in a very calm, respectful way. "It's just that. . . . you got so mad about something that wasn't only our fault. I know we were running late and I'm sorry, but you were running late, too. You weren't ready either, but we're the ones getting lectured. Didn't we all do the same thing, make the same mistake, including you?"

Busted.

Sometimes I wish I had raised dumber kids. Kids who would be oblivious to truth. Airheads. Puppets who would just nod and agree. But I digress. My boy was right. And my big, fat ego didn't like hearing it.

I tell my children daily, "I love you." I say those words when I'm the happiest with them and when I'm the angriest. I say them a lot. A lot, a lot. We're told constantly by experts and books and Oprah and cheesy Facebook posts that it's important to say those words to your children and for them to really believe them. I completely agree. But there are three words that when strung together can be even more powerful (though not more important) than "I love you."

Those words are "I am sorry."

Not a flippant "I am sorry." Not tossed off in passing. Not

mumbled out of frustration. Not skipped over in a hurry. Not followed with a qualifying "but . . ." I'm talking about a real, genuine, humble "I am sorry."

That morning, I'm ashamed to admit, my first instinct was not to apologize but to defend myself. Thankfully, my brain and heart and common sense kicked in before I opened my big, prideful mouth. I pulled the car to the side of the road, looked my son in the eye, and said, "I am sorry. Please forgive me. I was so stressed-out, and instead of dealing with it in a mature way, I took it out on you and your sister. And that was wrong and completely unfair. You did not deserve that. I am sorry." His face instantly changed. My boy needed to hear that, and I owed him and his siblings that apology.

I wish I could say that morning was the first time I messed up, but it wasn't the fifth or even the hundredth. I've failed as a mother many times. I've hurt my kids' feelings. I've been selfish. I've forgotten. I've been late. I've been unfair. I've lost my cool. I've done all those things repeatedly. Unfortunately, I'll probably do some of them again. To pretend I didn't or won't is not only unhealthy but also detrimental to my children's development because it destabilizes their sense of right and wrong and tells them that being perceived as perfect is more important than being accountable.

"I am sorry" creates trust.

"I am sorry" builds respect.

"I am sorry" promotes humility.

"I am sorry" shows that everyone makes mistakes.

"I am sorry" teaches that admitting you're wrong isn't a sign of weakness.

And if we're being honest, a consistent, genuine "I love you" can't exist without a consistent, genuine "I am sorry."

I will screw up as a parent. But the biggest failure I could ever make is allowing my pride to be greater than my child's need to hear me admit I'm wrong when I'm wrong. Owning my mistakes and apologizing for them doesn't diminish my power as a parent. It increases it. Apologizing and being able to move forward also demonstrates resilience to my kids—that being wrong won't keep you from receiving love or deserving happiness. My children will learn nothing from me if I foolishly act as if I'm always right, but they will learn everything from me if I live my life as an honest, vulnerable, flawed human.

The words we choose matter, because words can help heal or words can inflict hurt. Some would argue that we've become too sensitive about words. And yet I bet you can remember almost all of the hurtful words that have been said to you in your life, by a parent or a sibling or a friend. We carry those words and it's hard to shake their implications. Over time we can atone for the careless things we've said in haste or anger, but we can never take them back. I need to teach my kids to use their words so I can understand where they are coming from when they open up to me, and I want to use my own words to make them feel safe and loved and valued and respected when they do. The things we say to one another have the power to bolster or break our relationships, so in the end, it's simple: words matter to me because people matter to me.

Fourteen

Empathy

You know that parenting moment when you triumphantly put all of your energy into planning a fun family evening and then one tiny little thing happens and propels everyone into a rotten mood? Yeah, so that's pretty much a regular occurrence in my home.

One evening, we were leaving to go bowling—an activity every family member had agreed to and was actually excited about. (Miracles do happen, people!) Ari had successfully put his shoes on the correct feet, Luka stopped playing Xbox without having to be asked three times to shut it down, Philip had the car keys in hand, and I had changed out of my Cookie Monster onesie into actual grown-up clothes so as not to embarrass my children too many times in one week. We were just waiting on Matea. But at the last minute, her favorite sweatshirt had gone missing.

She ran around the house, frustrated, looking for it every-where. I could feel my family's fragile camaraderie dissipating as we waited by the front door, our enthusiasm giving way to annoy-ance with every passing minute. One of us (not naming names but possibly an older brother) yelled something like, "Well, maybe you should pay attention to where you leave your stuff! Are you gonna die without it?" And then another family member (who might look and sound exactly like me) impatiently called out something like, "We don't have time for this, Matea! Let's go!" Every second that went by increased the eye-rolling, the heavy sighs of irritation, and the unnecessary sideline commentary. Fi-nally, after what felt like hours (but was probably only about ten minutes), Matea found her sweatshirt in the garage, where she'd been playing earlier, and we all got in the car to head to the bowl-ing alley. The mood of our family evening, which was initially very positive, had turned super negative.

And then my empathy kicked in. See, my empathy and I have something in common. We both show up fashionably late to events. During the lost sweatshirt event, it would have been nice to have had my empathy ring the doorbell a little early instead of after all the guests had left for the bowling alley, but at least it decided to eventually show its pretty face to help with the post-party cleanup. It didn't bail on me completely. With empathy by my side, it finally occurred to me to do what I try to teach my kids to do: put myself in the other person's shoes. What would I have needed in Matea's situation?

I would have needed understanding and help. What I would *not* have needed is to be told things I already knew: that I was making everyone wait; that this was my fault; that I was ruining the evening by holding everyone up. Over the course of my career in motherhood, I have missed quite a few teachable moments by unconsciously putting my own emotions and trivial distractions ahead of my number one priority: teaching my children how to live in a way that will make them better humans.

How much smarter would it have been if, instead of just standing there by the front door in frustration, I had looked at everyone and said, "We got this! So . . . Luka, you check the bathrooms. Philip, you check the living room and kitchen. Ari and I will check the backyard and the garage. Matea, you check the bedrooms. Let's go!" (Blasting some fun music while we all ran around the house would have been a nice added touch because, life tip: a good soundtrack can make any annoying or boring activity more fun.) I could have used that sweatshirt situation as an opportunity to show compassion and teach my children that we are a team and work together to help one another out. We all mess up, we misplace stuff sometimes, and when something is important to one of us, it's important to all of us. Instead, Matea's family just stood around, focused only on our individual wants and needs in that moment.

WHETHER YOU'RE FIVE (the age of my youngest) or forty (the age of yours truly), putting yourself in other people's shoes is difficult and tedious work. For Ari, it's hard because his five-year-old brain hasn't had much practice at this imaginative leap. For me? I can get lazy. It's much simpler to believe that I'm sage, omniscient, and always right, and it's so easy to be seduced by the feeling that anyone who disagrees with me or reacts to a situation differently than I would is stupid or misinformed. Choosing to interrogate my perspective in any way and really consider the experiences of the people around me not only threatens my ego—it's also inconveniently time consuming.

Yet I believe empathy is the most important skill human beings can learn, and it's one I am determined to cultivate in my kids and myself. Empathy is the mother of kindness and patience. When I'm able to truly understand where another person is coming from, I can easily forgive them and figure out what might help or comfort them. Empathy is a magical bucket that always seems to have some grace left in it—even when you and your husband have both had insanely stressful days at work and are exhausted, and all he can think to do is complain about some stupid thing like not having any counter space in the bathroom because it's completely overtaken by your crap, and all you want to do is scream: "I LOOK LIKE A HUNGOVER MUG SHOT VERSION OF MYSELF WITHOUT ALL THIS CRAP, AND YES, I'M A SUCKER FOR PRODUCTS THAT PROMISE TO MAKE ME LOOK RESTED AND DEWY. AND NO, THEY NEVER WORK, AND NO, I DON'T EVEN FULLY UNDERSTAND THE DIFFERENCE BETWEEN GREASY AND DEWY, BUT NOW THAT I'VE OVERPAID FOR THEM, WE'RE GONNA RIDE THIS ROCKET ALL THE WAY INTO THE GROUND!" And that's just one completely hypothetical example. Empathy throws a little grace your way, and you're able to understand how annoying it might be to have nowhere to put down the shaving razor when he's nicked himself and needs to deal with the bloody aftermath. So you take a deep breath and march yourself to the Container Store to start getting organized. (Or, more realistically, you artfully push all your crap over to your side of the sink and pretend it will actually stay there this time.)

If my kids want to build strong friendships, what's the most important thing I can teach them? Empathy. Because people of all ages like feeling understood and heard. If they want to be powerful CEOs? Empathy again. Because the best leaders connect with people and make them feel seen. If they want to make art, write books, or direct movies? You got it—empathy. Because you can't create convincingly or connect with audiences if you can't understand what motivates people. And if they want to be successful physicists? Well, they're just going to have to go to some kind of a summer physics camp for that, because this mama doesn't speak physics.

The more creative and participatory we make life lessons, the more they'll sink in and stick with us and our kids. Of course, actively going through a lesson is a lot more work than just lecturing, which you can add to the never-ending list of reasons I'm perpetually exhausted, a list that is now as lengthy as one of those three-mile-long CVS receipts.

There's an exercise I started having my older kids do when they argue that's been really helpful in my quest to raise empathetic future members of society. When they disagree, I make them switch roles and argue the other person's perspective (and not sarcastically). Luka has to take Matea's side and try to convince her that she's right while Matea takes on Luka's perspective and tries to sell him on his convictions.

One afternoon we were driving home from school and Luka and Matea were going at it over the stereo again. Matea's an

Adele and Taylor Swift fan while Luka's tastes tend more toward harder-rock bands and rap.

"Nope, nope, nope," I called back over their bickering. "Switch roles."

"But, Mom!" my kids groaned.

"Either you two switch roles or I'm practicing karaoke."

"Ugh, fine!" They rolled their eyes.

Luka started by arguing Matea's views. "I think that it's stressful to listen to music where it sounds like everyone's angry and shouting."

"Well, sometimes when you're frustrated, it feels really good to hear someone else let it all out," Matea replied.

"I can understand how it might be comforting to listen to someone sing about mean girls when you're dealing with them at school. Plus your voice is high-pitched, so it's easier for you to sing along to other high-pitched, girly voices," Luka countered.

"Maybe they use curse words in the songs you listen to because . . . they just don't know that many words?" Matea said with a half smile. Luka snorted. And then they both ended up laughing.

It's amazing what happens when they are forced to argue a point they might disagree with. Suddenly they have access to where the other person might be coming from and *why* they think the way they do. Not only is it a wonderful way to build and flex their empathy muscles, but it often leaves both kids cracking up at the absurdity of the whole argument in the first place.

Once I noticed how well this role reversal worked for my kids, I decided to try it with Philip when we have silly marital arguments, and it's become our new favorite way to solve dis-agreements. No one leaves the conflict feeling pissed off or un-heard, it helps us understand each other better, and, most of the time, the discussion ends with laughter instead of anger.

When Luka was in elementary school, empathy often seemed to come naturally to him. He came home one day from second grade and asked me if I could take him to the store to buy a bracelet for a girl at school.

"Luka! That's so sweet! Do you have a little crush on her?"

"No. I don't even really know her. It's just that some kids were picking on her and one kid grabbed her arm and her bracelet fell off and broke. She needs a new bracelet as soon as possible. She didn't ask for it, but I just know it would help her feel better."

The following day, Luka gave the girl a cute little bracelet with green plastic beads that he'd picked out himself. He didn't think of it as a big deal. He just thought it was the right thing to do. And I couldn't have been prouder of him, especially since he wasn't always so in tune with how his actions might be perceived.

But his empathy development had its ups and downs. When Luka was around six years old, he went through a phase of being extremely curious about death and dying. I explained to him that people die for various reasons, but most people live long lives, and only when they get really old is it their time to go. Around this time, a dear friend of mine in her fifties came for a visit to escape the drama she had going on at home. Her husband had recently left her for a twentysomething. She'd had the same gor-geous skin all of the years I'd known her, and now had chic gray hair that she didn't fuss with. As we were all hanging out in the

living room, Luka suddenly asked my friend, "How old are you?"
I gently explained to him that even though people ask him how
old he is, it's not polite for him to ask adults how old they are (a
sentiment I don't totally agree with, but that's a rant for another
day). Luka looked my friend straight in the eye and said, in all
earnestness, "Oh, I'm sorry. I didn't mean to be rude, it's just that
you look *so old*. Like you're going to die *right now*."

I wanted to die *right now*. From utter humiliation! In fact,
nothing sounded better at that moment than my dying *right now*.

Luka's statement would have been hurtful if it had been di-
rected at anyone, but he was saying this to a woman whose husband had just replaced her with someone half her age! My friend
tried to laugh it off, while I awkwardly, talking faster than an
auctioneer, tried to apologize/compliment/somehow make it better, until I realized shutting up would probably be the best course
of action. Luka didn't mean any harm by what he said, it's just
really hard for a six-year-old to understand that gray hair doesn't
mean you're ancient or to empathize with the idea of aging as
something to be embarrassed about. (Honestly, I still have a hard
time wrapping my head around why our culture turns getting
older into such a negative.) Obviously, he had yet to master the
art of empathy or even dip a toe into the practice. But during
those young years, he tried. He really tried to be empathetic.

When Luka was seven years old, during one of his soccer
games, he bumped into another kid and the kid fell down. At half-
time, as I was passing out the obligatory orange slices, I pulled
him aside and said, "Hey, if you bump into someone and they fall
down, give them a hand to help them up. It's just a nice thing to
do and you'd appreciate it if someone did that for you. Okay?"

My dear son spent the rest of the game running around the field helping up *every single* player who fell down. And when seven-year-olds are playing soccer, there's a *lot* of falling down! He wasn't just helping the kids on his team. No, no. He was helping up the kids on the other team as well! The coach was annoyed, the parents looked confused, and Philip was chuckling and giving me the "See what you did!?!" look. I just stood there, slightly uncomfortable with the chaos I had caused, yet wearing the cheesiest grin on my face. I broke into laughter every time my kid booked it across the field to help yet another kid up. By the end of the game, Luka had played the least amount of soccer of anyone on the field, but he was completely out of breath from running back and forth like a crazy person to help his fallen comrades.

Then the preteen years hit and my thoughtful son suddenly became a lot more self-centered. We all get caught up in ourselves at times, whether we want to admit it or not, but during those teenage years everything becomes all about *you* and how hard and terrible life is. As much as seeing my sweet boy turn into a brooding, hormonal monster made me want to tear my hair out, I also really felt for him. As I watched Luka become more and more consumed with himself and his problems, I wondered how I could help him out of his funk. Yapping at him about it wouldn't help much. I needed something proactive, something that would lead him to his own epiphany.

I didn't have to reach as far back as my own teenage years to relate to my son's self-absorbed despair; I'd been there myself following my divorce. I knew exactly what it was like to become so obsessed with your misery that the gravitational center of the world shifts to revolve entirely around you. And I also knew that

I could pull myself free from that sinkhole only when I deliberately focused on helping others.

When I spend one-on-one time with each of my children, I find they open up and tell me things that I probably wouldn't hear about if our whole family was sitting at the dinner table together. I made plans to spend time with Luka one evening and spent all day racking my brain for something new we could do that would help him reorient his perspective to include others. When we got in the car that night I said, "We're going to do something different today. Instead of just going to a restaurant for dinner, we're going to play a game."

Luka immediately rolled his eyes, because any game that a mother suggests to her teenager is bound to be lame and "for old people." But I decided not to take the eye-rolling personally. His boy eyes were turning into man eyes, and the only way they could do that is if they rolled back and forth, usually in my presence. It's science.

I continued, "Here's the game. We have two hours to complete three random acts of kindness. No plan! We just drive around and look for three things we can do to help someone out or make someone's day."

Luka responded with a few more manly eye-development exercises. "Yeah, okay, whatever, but I'm really hungry."

We started off by hitting up his favorite fast-food restaurant. As we went through the drive-through, a car pulled up behind us. "There's our first act!" I said excitedly. "We're going to pay for their meal." When we got to the window to pay our bill, we told the cashier we wanted to wait for the car behind us to order so that we could cover their meal, too. As we waited, Luka's face changed. This *was* exciting! Not lame. As soon as we finished paying and were handed our burgers and fries, I peeled out of the parking lot.

"Mom, we can't just drive off! We need to stick around and see the person's reaction!"

Now it was my turn to roll my eyes at him. "Trust me, their reaction will be good! Who doesn't appreciate a free meal? But if you're going to be honest, are you wanting to stick around because you want praise from them? We all enjoy compliments. We all enjoy getting credit for the things we do. But are we willing to go out of our way to do something without waiting for the recognition?"

I knew that there would be many times in Luka's life when he wouldn't get the pat on the back he deserved. Doing something nice for another person could be its own reward, and if I could show Luka how to feel that—really feel it—I knew he'd be equipped with a new emotional tool that would help him lead a happier life.

After our first random act of kindness, we drove around and chatted until we passed a laundromat, which got us talking about how awesome it is that we have a washer and a dryer in our home, and how it's something that we take for granted. We decided to turn around and head back to the laundromat, but first we stopped at a gas station to change a five-dollar bill into quarters. When we got to the parking lot, I said, "I want *you* to do it. I want you to walk into the laundromat, and I want you to pick somebody—whoever you want—and just hand them the pile of coins."

Luka hesitated. "I don't know . . ." he said.

"Just go in and whoever strikes you, whoever stands out to

you, just go and hand this money to them. But before you go, I need you to remember something important. Just because we are lucky enough to have a laundry machine in our home right now does not make you superior to someone who doesn't. Fortunes change all the time, but every human life has the same value— always. So whoever you give these coins to, you look that person in the eye the way you look at your friends, the way you look at me, the way you want to be looked at—with respect, as an equal. Got it?" Luka nodded, took a deep breath, and hopped out of the car.

Inside the laundromat, he saw a woman struggling with the coin machine. It kept spitting her dollar bills back out and she seemed frustrated. He walked over to her, stretched out his hand filled with the quarters, and said, "This is for you." She looked up at him, confused.

"What?"

"This is for you."

"But why?" she asked.

He looked back at me, and I gave him the nod—*go ahead, just give it to her.*

"My mom and I really want you to have this. For no reason. We just want you to have it."

The woman's eyes welled up with tears, and I saw Luka's face soften again. A small act of kindness could make a big difference in someone's day.

He got back in the car, and as we were driving away, I kept thinking, *Okay, we paid for somebody's dinner and we paid for somebody's laundry. But I want to teach my kids that kindness and*

*thoughtfulness don't require money. I want them to know that you don't
have to have a lot to give a lot.* We drove around and around until
we noticed a store parking lot full of scattered carts. (Because,
apparently, people are just too busy to take the necessary ten
seconds to return their carts to the designated spot.) I parked the
car and said, "This is our next mission. We're going to clean up
this lot!"

Luka protested. "But, Mom, that's somebody's job. Somebody
gets paid to do that!"

"That's fine. We're just going to help them out. If you had a
job, wouldn't you love it if someone randomly showed up to make
your day a little easier? Maybe that person would normally have
to stay and work late, and maybe now they'll get to go home a
little earlier."

We got out of the car and returned every cart—about two
dozen of them. Right as we were finishing up, a kid who didn't
look much older than Luka came out of the store, saw the pristine
parking lot, and said, "Wow. I was going to have to put all those
carts back tonight, and it's my least favorite part of my job. I can't
believe you guys just did this! Thank you so much."

This game is now on regular rotation in our family's activi-
ties, and not just with the kids. Sometimes my husband and I do
it on a date night. There's so much in this smartphone-centric
world that nudges us further and further into self-absorption. I
want to raise my children to notice the world and the people
around them and consider how the way they move through their
lives has the power to make other people's lives better or worse.
Beyond just teaching reactionary kindness, beyond teaching my

kids to help others who ask, I want to teach my kids to actively look for those who are hurting, those who are in need.

Sometimes real help can be as simple as a kind word. Or letting someone go ahead of us in line, or walking by a meter that's about to expire and throwing some change in, or writing a letter to a former teacher who made a difference in our life. Sometimes it's just looking someone in the eye when they're sitting on the street, somebody who feels alone and isolated, who is treated like they are not so much a person as an unsavory obstacle.

Did our random acts of kindness cure my teenager of his self-absorption? No. Did it make me immune to self-absorption? Of course not. We will always struggle to balance caring for others with focusing on ourselves. Our own problems will still seduce us from time to time, but embracing creative ways to yank the gaze from our own navels and redirect our eyeballs outward moves us toward the people we aspire to be. Doing one sit-up won't give me six-pack abs (boo! hiss!), so our empathy workout can't be just a onetime thing either. We must make empathy practice part of our daily lives.

Last year, I got to work with Andre Agassi, which was one of those pinch-me moments and still feels like an insane thing to be able to say. In addition to being a world-famous tennis legend, Andre is also a dad. As we were chatting about our families, we got to talking about parenting teenagers and he said something that really stuck with me: "We raise our children for about fourteen years, and then we just mitigate risk."

We only have a dozen or so years to instill in our children the core values we hope will guide them through the rest of their lives. After that, our influence wanes and their independence blossoms. We never really ever stop parenting, but our years of intense influence eventually fade, kind of like how our body's ability to quickly metabolize desserts fades once we hit middle age (P.S. still very pissed about this). Knowing that it's natural for our power and influence to diminish doesn't necessarily make the transition any easier, especially when a teenager stretching their wings can often feel more like someone just whacking you in the face repeatedly.

Sometimes I think of my son Luka as wearing a mask: a mask made of hormones, social pressures, and stress instead of papier-mâché, paint, and string. I have to trust that the son I raised is still there underneath, and that, eventually, the mask will come off and I'll get to look at the face of the man I raised. In the meantime, I take comfort in the little flashes I see of the boy who once gave a girl a bracelet just to be kind, and try to remember how very difficult it is to walk in a sixteen-year-old's shoes.

Fifteen

Kids First, Ego Last

My ex-husband slept over. Then, in the morning, my current husband and my ex chatted in the kitchen about football and how equally awful their teams were. As we prepared for breakfast, Ari chased my ex with a toy leaf blower while Philip helped Matea put the presents she made for everyone under the tree. Luka was back and forth between both men, debating Nirvana versus Pearl Jam. It was Christmas morning, and if aliens had stopped by my house for a visit, they would have thought that postdivorce parenting here on earth is a piece of cake.

Postdivorce coparenting is not a piece of cake, though. It's a large, week-old, seven-layer bean dip made of complications, stress, disagreements, bitterness, scheduling conflicts, compromises, and crap. Divorce sucks. When I left my first marriage, things were ugly. I was bitter; he was bitter. I was hurt; he was hurt. Finding my voice in the middle of that tornado was excruciating. But ending the marriage wasn't anywhere nearly as hard as figuring out how to coparent after our divorce.

Although it seemed impossible at first, I was committed to giving my kids the best possible "growing up with divorced parents" scenario. Before the divorce was finalized, but after we were separated, my ex would drop by to pick up the kids for the weekend. We wouldn't say a word to each other. Not one word. It was as if we both knew that if we even dared to open our mouths, something ugly was bound to come out.

He couldn't stand me and I couldn't stand him, but even more so, I couldn't stand our venom. I knew that even though our kids were young and we were careful not to let them hear us bicker, our silence would inevitably poison them if we didn't figure out how to be around each other in a more amicable way. We *had* to make this better.

If we'd been able to give our kids a choice, I'm sure they would have preferred to grow up with parents who were together and in love. I knew, though, that in the long run it would be better for my children if their dad and I weren't together, but getting to the end of the long run wouldn't be easy or painless for them. My job was to take the crappy situation they were in and create the best possible scenario out of it. The task seemed daunting, so I started at what seemed like the most obvious place, with the only two people in the world who had almost as much impact on my kids' lives as their mom and dad did—I started with their grandparents. My parents lived far away, in Croatia, so I got in my car and drove four hours north to visit my ex-husband's parents for a very blunt conversation.

We sat together at their dining table, the same table where

we'd met for the first time years ago when I was hoping they'd approve of me as their son's girlfriend. I felt much more nervous now and had a lot more at stake, hoping they'd accept me as their son's ex-wife.

I took a deep breath and reminded myself that I wasn't there to convince them that things were irreconcilable between me and their son or to get them to take my side in the divorce. I wasn't there to talk in circles, to rehash our anger and frustration. I was there to talk about the only question we could unanimously agree was important and in our collective power to address: How do we make this easiest on the kids? How do we do what is best for Luka and Matea?

We talked for hours, late into the night. My ex-in-laws were incredibly gracious, more gracious than I might have been in their situation. I was in awe of their ability to set their own disappointments aside and treat me with such kindness. There was a lot of sadness and they reiterated their stance that I should stay with their son and try to make the marriage work. But they did so respectfully and promised that no matter what, they would do all they could to keep things amicable between all of us for their grandchildren. Our conversation ended with a sentiment that meant even more to me than the welcome they extended to me as a girlfriend years back. As we said goodbye, they told me, "Well, if you're no longer our daughter-in-law, then from now on, you are our daughter."

I expected them to dislike me. I expected them to judge my choices. I expected their anger to burn me, searing me like hot coals. Instead, they showed me unconditional love—the most unexpected and profound gift they could have possibly offered me at that time.

They have actively kept up their end of this deal. They still invite me over for family gatherings. They call me just to check in or to tell me that they were thinking about me. They send me thoughtful gifts and encouraging cards. For the first few years after the divorce, my ex-husband visited his parents with the kids almost every weekend. While they were there, his mom would call me to keep me updated, to ask for a favorite recipe so that she could make it for the kids, or to check if I had any new techniques to share with her for getting a stubborn toddler to poop in the toilet. When the weekend was over, she'd send the kids home to me with a batch of her famous Ultimate Chocolate Bars. My ex's parents always praised me in front of the kids and didn't add drama to their lives. I don't take any of this for granted. To have all parties involved focused on making a painful divorce unusually amicable—and, sadly, it *is* unusual—every single adult in our family had to put their egos aside. Not easy. But so worth it.

On the drive home after my long conversation with my ex-husband's parents, I came up with a personal formula for how I aspired to handle the many difficult situations that lay ahead: Kids first, ego last. I wrote it down on a Post-it and stuck it to my bathroom mirror as a constant reminder. I wrote it on a small piece of paper and tucked it into my wallet. I asked my closest friends to keep me accountable to it. I was scaling a formidable mountain of bitterness and pride and knew I was too out of shape to make it to the other side alone. I owed it to my kids to try, so I strapped on hiking boots and started climbing that sucker, step by uncertain step, taking it one day at a time. Before every meeting with my ex, I'd whisper my new mantra to myself: *Kids first, ego last.*

Too often we wait until we start feeling differently before we begin evolving the way we act toward those we don't get along with. But I know that how I behave can dictate how I feel. So even though I was still mad at my ex (and he was mad at me), I decided to try doing something I'd do if I actually did get along with him. One Father's Day not long after our divorce, I made up a basket full of foods I knew he liked, and when he came to my apartment to get the kids, Luka ran up and said, "Look, Daddy, we made you a picnic!"

I also started inviting him over for dinner. The first few times he said no, and then . . . he said yes. Slowly, I was starting to see that treating my ex with kindness was making me *feel* kinder toward him. And I know it made Luka's and Matea's lives just a little less complicated to have two parents who, while they might not have been married any longer, could at least break bread and marvel at the amazing children they'd brought into this world together.

As we were struggling through the emotional turmoil and murkiness of coparenting, we also had to learn how to handle all the postdivorce logistics. That juggling act alone would be enough to overwhelm anybody. Divorce shakes up daily routines in innumerable ways, and it is hard to figure out how best to provide kids with a sense of stability in a sea of changes.

My children spend most weekends with their dad, who sometimes has different rules than I do and runs his home on a different schedule. On Sundays, the kids return to me. For a long time, I expected them to immediately fit right back into my way of running things. If one of them forgot something important, like a school assignment or a sports uniform, at their dad's house,

I'd get annoyed. If they did something that was acceptable at their dad's house but not at mine, I'd get irritated and proceed to lecture them.

I didn't even realize how unfair this was to my children. Then one of them pointed out how confusing and complicated it was to live in two different homes. Here I thought I was doing everything I could to shield my kids from the negative effects of divorce, but I needed to focus on more than just the emotional stuff. I needed to spread the empathy to more practical areas as well.

That's when I came up with "jet lag day." You know how when you come home after a trip across time zones, you need a little time to acclimate before you feel like yourself again? I decided that my children deserved time to adjust from one home to the other, from one parent to the other. So every Monday became jet lag day, a day of extra, *extra* mercy and grace. This didn't mean that my kids could get away with acting like total demons on Mondays, but I would do my best to be extra patient and understanding as they readjusted to life in my house. Jet lag day has made the dynamic shifts in my kids' days less stressful and much more manageable for all of us.

A few years after the divorce, as I was driving Luka to kindergarten, completely out of the blue he surprised me with, "Mom, I figured out the real reason Daddy and you got divorced." My heart sank.

"How did you figure out the real reason, Luka?" I asked.

"Oh, just something I heard at Daddy's house."

Anger kicked in. As I was trying to figure out how I was going to respond to whatever bomb my son was about to drop on me, my thoughts got interrupted by Luka. "Cheese!" he yelled from the backseat.

"What?"

"Cheese, Mom! Daddy said he hates cheese. He hates all the cheeses in the whole wide world. And you love cheese. A lot! More than is normal. So of course you couldn't stay married. I couldn't be married to someone who hated Legos!"

I smiled, flooded with relief. And then I said, "You know, Luka, you're a really smart guy. And though cheese isn't the real reason Daddy and I got divorced, it is true that sometimes two people just don't make a great match. It's kind of like trying to put two puzzle pieces together that don't fit. You can wiggle them around, push them together, and try really hard to make them fit, but they just won't. Daddy and I were kind of like those puzzle pieces. We couldn't fit. We tried."

Every time the kids broached the subject of our family's divorce, it felt so right in my soul to be able to answer their questions without putting their dad down or pointing fingers. One day when Matea was six, a friend of hers came over for a playdate. As I walked by her bedroom to check on them, I overheard her tell her friend, "My mom and dad are really good friends!" I got choked up. My little girl meant that. She really thought that my ex-husband and I were close friends. We're not, but the fact that my sweet girl believed this gave me such peace. I've heard so many kids and adults from divorced homes talk about how much their parents hate each other, how they can't even be in the same room together, how they're worried about the drama their divorced parents might cause at important events like graduation ceremonies and weddings. And here was my little girl, not in the ideal situation, but not seeing her mom and dad as each other's enemies.

My ex and I go to parent-teacher conferences and school performances together. At soccer games, we sit near each other so that our children won't have to feel pulled in two different directions when they look to make sure their parents saw them score that goal. We work to avoid putting our kids in the unfair position of having to choose sides between us. Whenever I feel the urge to indulge my ego, I ask myself, *Is this what's really best for my children, or will this just make* me *feel temporarily better?* Oh, I hate it when I ask myself that question. I hate it more than early mornings and exercise and paper cuts and the dentist. But I choose to deal with this question daily, from the way I treat my ex-husband in front of our kids to the way I word my texts or emails to him. Even though my kids will never read those words, they still matter, because they inform the tone of our relationship.

Recently, as I parked my car at our local library, I saw a man crouching down, two little kids wrapped in his arms. They looked like they were holding on to him so tightly. Tears started running down my cheeks. I recognized the scene playing out here. I could tell what was happening, and as I scanned the parking lot, I saw a woman standing nearby, facing the man and the children but looking down at the pavement. The man said something to his children and then they walked toward the woman and embraced her, still throwing glances back at their dad, as if they were torn. They were. The man stood up and kept his gaze focused on the kids. Even though I was a good distance away, I could sense the sadness. A family broken. Parents each in their corner. Kids pulled between them, sad to let go of one parent but happy to embrace the other. As I cried, my gaze still stuck on these four strangers, I wondered if they would ever get to a place where they could spend time together as a family. Would they always feel broken? Is it possible for divorce, though it may initially break a family, to actually strengthen those relationships, like a bone that needs to be reset in order to heal? I don't know the answer, but that's the silent prayer I said for that family, and the hope I have for my own.

Divorce is never easy and always complicated, and I want to make one thing clear: the arrangement I have with my ex will not work for every family. If your ex or a member of your extended family threatens you or your children's safety, for example, you do *not* have to keep them in your life. None of my advice applies in any of those extreme situations. But when there are innocent kids involved, we owe it to them to remember that they didn't ask for any of this heartache and our drama is not their responsibility.

After I met Philip and our relationship got serious enough that I realized I could spend the rest of my life with him, I knew that he, too, would have to put his ego aside and put the kids first if he was going to be a part of our family. I also had to accept that if he couldn't put his ego aside when it came to my ex, it wouldn't mean he was a terrible person, it would actually mean he was a very normal person—a normal person with whom I would have to choose to part ways. It would have broken my heart to end this amazing thing I had going with Philip, but I knew that the amazing thing wouldn't last very long if we weren't all on the same page.

Just like with every conversation I've had with Philip since our first date, I chose the brutally blunt approach when broaching the topic of my ex. I always assumed that if I spelled it all out honestly and he ran, I would wish him well and not chase after him. (That's a good tactic with any relationship: show them the crap first! And then let them decide if they want to handle your crap, instead of blindsiding them with the crap once they're already all in.) So I sat Philip down and dove in: "You know how much I love my children, and that means I need to do everything I can to create a drama-free environment for them . . . which means that I'll probably choose to cater to my ex sometimes. I will do everything in my power to make sure we can all be together for special occasions and holidays so that the kids don't feel divided. I will make a big deal for him for Father's Day and for his birthday. I will never say one bad thing about him in front of my children. I will always make him feel welcome in my home, even having him over for dinner occasionally so that the kids can have all of us together at times. I realize that asking you to be okay with all of that is a lot, and I also understand if you think it seems completely ludicrous and unreasonable, but this isn't something I can compromise on. So if you have issues with any of that, or maybe jealousy, I completely understand. To be honest, I don't know if I could do what I'm asking of you, but I'm trying desperately to do what I feel is best for my children. And I would rather be single for the rest of my life than be with a man who would stand in the way of my creating a peaceful, united environment for my family. I'm not expecting you to agree to any of this. I'm just letting you know that if you want to be a part of my life, my ex will have to be a part of your life. So . . . I guess this is the moment where you politely dump me."

Philip didn't dump me. He knew that my actions didn't mean

I harbored romantic feelings for my ex. I knew that this was still going to be a challenge for him. Thankfully, it was a challenge he was willing to tackle.

Soon after this conversation, Philip accompanied me to drop my kids off at my ex-husband's apartment. As we were leaving, he overheard my ex say something about needing to move a dishwasher but not knowing anyone with a truck who could help him. Philip quickly blurted out, "I know someone with a truck! When do you need him?"

"Saturday morning," my ex replied.

"Yep, you got it!" Philip responded. "We'll be there!"

Philip didn't actually know anyone with a truck. As we started walking away, he began feverishly texting his friends, Anyone know someone with a truck? He saw this moment as an opportunity to show my ex that he wasn't there to compete with him. The gesture immediately set the tone for their relationship and, eventually, led to us hanging out together with the kids, Philip getting to know my ex's parents and celebrating Thanksgiving at their house every year, and even attending church together, sometimes sitting all in a row: my three kids, my two husbands, and me.

THERE'S ONE IMPORTANT PART of this postdivorce story that I can't tell, and that's what it's like to be a stepparent. I can't speak to the experience of stepparenting because I've never walked in those shoes. But luckily, I have an expert nearby: my husband, Philip. I'll hand off the rest of this chapter to him.

I still remember the day I met her. I still remember how beautiful she was and how the whole room seemed to stop when she walked in. I remember the tension of the few months before we began dating, and that she seemed to be full of energy all of the time. I could never have imagined then how much she would change my life, how much she would teach me about love and growth, and how much she would make me laugh. I remember the day she first introduced me to her daughter. I could never have imagined on that day that this little, precious child would one day call me Dad and that it would be all I needed to have a great day. I remember when her little boy walked up to me and asked if I was going to marry his mommy, and all I could think about was how lucky I would be if that were to happen. I could never have imagined on that day that this little guy would one day come to me with his most personal problems, searching for answers, and that I would never feel more important or proud than when he walked away feeling better. The three of them transformed my world and opened my eyes. I can't think of what my days were like before them and how empty they must have been, not filled with little kisses and little hugs and tender care from someone who truly puts you first.

And now I'm a stepdad. The word elicits so many thoughts, feelings, stereotypes, and expectations. Being a stepdad is a wonderful blessing, but it is also a loaded word. I honestly still feel a little weird saying it to people. It feels like somehow I am almost a dad, but just not quite. Like I've passed all the tests, but I missed a few credits of PE and so didn't get my diploma. Sometimes I feel like a kicker in football. Sure, I'm on an NFL team, and yeah, we won the Super Bowl, but . . . And no offense to any kickers out there. I have the utmost respect for their ability to function under such amazing stress and pressure. But I think in some ways stepparenting is not so different. Most of the time I defer to the kids' father, but there are those pressure-packed moments when the game is on the line and I have to perform as if I have been out there the whole time. And that transition needs to be seamless so that the kids have stability. That's really what it's all about, isn't it? The kids. I told Kristina before we got married that I felt like I was marrying three people, and that wasn't me just being cheesy. It was the truth, and I am so thankful I was able to see that ahead of time.

My first and biggest piece of advice to any person considering marrying someone who has a child is to wrap your head around the idea that you are marrying a family and not just a spouse. Certainly, every situation is different depending on the status of the other parent and the ages of the children, but the truth remains: you *are* marrying all of them. They may or may not be "your kids," but they are your family, and you need to do everything you possibly can to convey your commitment to them so they feel the same way about you. The biggest challenge for me has been throwing myself fully into the role of "dad," right up until the second their father walks in the door, and then being able to take an immediate step back. I love, more than anything, being their dad and parenting is such a central part of how I define myself now. Stepparenting is such a fine line to walk and it takes an awful lot of patience and self-restraint to take off that hat at any given moment. I am nowhere close to perfect at this, but I always come back to thinking about the kids and their stability first. They need to know that I will keep them safe and take care of them in every way and that I am their fearless leader and defender and love them with all of my heart. But I also need to make it clear that there isn't a power struggle between their father and me, that he and I are on the same team, and that I am in no way replacing or trying to get ahead of him. If you want to make sure the kids aren't playing you against each other, then show them at all times that you are working together. Clearly this doesn't work when the father is someone who should not be a role model to the kids, is abusive to them, or has serious issues.

As stepparents, we are often set up to fail. Stepparents walk into a situation with a complicated history and have so many relationships to juggle and understand. We aren't psychologists who can recognize the underlying fears and deep neuroses that shape how someone may respond to a simple request, like "Please pass the salt." The best you can hope for is to build trust and show love and strength. Those tenets have to guide how you interact with your stepchildren's father, too. You have to show him that his children are first on your priority list, ahead of any of the ego issues we all deal with. I helped Kristina's ex-husband move a dishwasher a few weeks after I first met him. He hadn't asked, but I overheard them discussing it and I offered. Was it a little awkward? Sure (maybe even more for him than for me). But I wanted to establish from the beginning that I was there to help him in any way I could because we would be in this together for a very long time, assuming I could convince that cute, curly-haired Croatian girl to stick around. I needed her to know that I was willing to do anything to make our relationship work because I knew we had something really good. I also invited her ex-husband over the first time the kids watched *Star Wars*. I was so excited for them to see it, but I also felt like he should be there for this big moment in their lives. I mean, it's *Star Wars*! So we watched, one kid next to him on one couch and the other next to me. And they switched spots a number of times throughout the movie. I didn't feel deprived in any way because he was there and I know the kids felt like they got more. It's that type of thing that makes me truly happy. I continue to go out of my way for him. He, in turn, has been good about including me in things and helping me out whenever he can. Sure, many bizarre conversations and situations have arisen, but I keep telling myself: this is bigger than me.

I push my pride aside, I swallow a few weird scenarios, and the kids think our family dynamics are totally normal. They have no idea about all the drama and mess this whole stepdad thing is "supposed" to cause. Maybe we can redefine what normal is, which seems especially valuable given that the current normal sucks. Our normal, after a few years of both their dad and me going out of our way, means doing our best to never make anyone feel excluded. I have always given the kids the choice to call me Philip or Dad. When they choose to call me Dad, it makes my heart melt. They go through phases and I never take what they offer for granted. But I also correct them anytime they call their father by his first name. He is always "Dad." He gets that honor; I have to earn it. And that is something I really like about being a stepdad. They get to choose how they feel about me. Thankfully, my two older kids choose to love me and that makes being "not quite a dad" pretty fantastic.

Being a kicker probably isn't so bad either. If you hit that last-second field goal to win the Super Bowl, the fans will remember you forever. But the likelihood of your success comes from how you practice every day of the season when no one seems to be paying you any attention.

Sixteen

Raw Kale and
Sprinkle Donuts

I broke down in public recently. I was in a packed restaurant, sitting across from my mother-in-law, who had accompanied me for a check-in about how one of her grandchildren was doing. At the moment, she was waiting—beaming warmth and compassion my way—as I mustered the strength to utter just one cohesive sentence about our situation. And then I completely lost it. I cried into my spinach dip and a plate of potato skins. Because parenting can break us.

Motherhood is the most heart-filling part of my life, and it is also at times the most heartbreaking. Recently, I have been really struggling watching one of my children struggle. I've been trying every trick I know, rushing to learn the skills I need but don't yet have, shoving aside the temptation to slide into naïve bliss, exhausting myself trying to fix what I can, and holding myself back from doing too much. Yet at the end of every day I am left feeling like all of my effort was useless. This is an excruciating place to be.

But here's the crazy revelation I've also had: I don't feel guilty. I don't feel inadequate. Let's be honest—feeling guilty and inadequate is par for the course when it comes to the extreme sport that is parenting. In the past when I've felt overwhelmed by the demands of this crazy gig and without a clue as to where to look for the answers I need, guilty and inadequate feelings have always been right there waiting for me with open arms.

The biggest lesson I've learned while wrestling with these new struggles is that parenting is in big part about simply showing up. Even when we feel overwhelmed and clueless, we have to show up. And as long as I'm showing up, how dare I berate myself? I have to show up for the tough stuff, but it is just as important that I show up for the fun stuff, even when the fun is hard to find. As much as I hate the word "balance" when it comes to describing the ways we attempt to juggle all of our responsibilities (in that case, it is a dirty word!), I love the word "balance" when it comes to my parenting philosophy: My mission is to find the balance between strict and fun.

I GUESS IN SOME WAYS, I approach parenting the way I approach eating. I believe in a balance between giving my body the nutrients it needs to feel good and full of energy—so I make sure leafy greens like kale are in regular rotation on my plate—but I also indulge in foods that bring me bliss. A donut with rainbow sprinkles may not be high in nutritional value but it is exceptionally high in joy-3 and delight-6, which are important ingredients in my sanity multivitamin. Being miserable is bad for my health. So when it comes to parenting, I try to be a strict parent who teaches common sense, follows through, and helps my kids see the value even in doing tasks they don't always enjoy. But I also try to encourage fun and spontaneity, and strive to help them find joy in the mundane parts of life. Kale and sprinkle donuts; my well-being requires both.

Our house is full of laughter. We're goofy and dorky and ridiculous. I prank my kids. Often. We have dance parties. Sometimes at Target. My kids get dessert every single day. Occasionally dessert ends with me smearing cake all over their faces. We celebrate everything. We celebrate nothing. I've been known to throw my kids "We're proud of you!" parties—not after a great report card or a perfectly cleaned room but for no reason at all. Or, actually, sometimes for the most important reason: because I saw them behave in a thoughtful, compassionate way.

My kids also have responsibilities. The older two have been doing their own laundry since they were ten years old, and the youngest one will start at that age as well. They have bedtimes. They pack most of their school lunches. They help with household tasks. My kids don't get paid for basic chores. They do chores because they're part of the family and therefore part of a team that works together to make our home run smoothly. They don't get an allowance either. Nothing. Not a single buck. Because one of my main jobs as a parent is to prepare them for real life, and in real life you don't get money just because you're alive. No one shows up at my door and hands me cash once a week.

Money is earned. If they want money, they do extra chores, for which they are compensated.

When I give a consequence, I follow through. Even if doing so complicates my day. Though my kids would never believe me, we parents know that consequences can be as annoying and inconvenient for us as they are for the kids. I once took my high schooler's phone away for more than seven months. Annoying for me? Absolutely, because I couldn't reach him as easily when I needed to; but it had to be done. I've canceled parties, opted out of a movie premiere I was looking forward to attending, and shelved entire trips just so that my kids could see I was true to my word. When I say, "If you do this, such-and-such will happen," such-and-such *will* happen, and they will hate such-and-such because I am really good at coming up with terrible such-and-suches.

I believe I can give my children a fun, full life and still lay down the law when I need to. I can give them lots of great memories without giving in to their every demand. I believe I can encourage them to talk openly with me about anything and not succumb to condoning their every whim. I believe I can empower my children without giving them power to rule over me. The way I see it, my job is to be the rule enforcer but also the fun enforcer. Working to implement and constantly adjust those two elements to achieve balance not only helps my children thrive but also helps me enjoy parenting.

Parenting is not like riding a bike. Just because you mastered one facet of the job with one kid does not mean you'll have a clue how to handle the next one—or even the next obstacle that comes your way. Because the next kid might not be a bike. He might be a tractor. And you've probably never tried to operate a tractor before! I don't believe that the same punishment applied to different people will yield the same results, just like I don't believe that privileges should automatically kick in at preset ages. I know some thirteen-year-olds who are mature enough to use social media and some fortysomethings who aren't. Whether it's a consequence or an incentive, I try to tailor my response to the individual. (I doubt my children appreciate how exhausting it is to put in this extra effort, but perhaps you, dear reader, will.) I also make a point of leaving consequences open-ended. If, for instance, I've taken the phone away from one of my kids, I don't say they can have it back on Saturday if they're good. I want phone privileges to be earned through a pattern of positive behavior, not by a spate of good actions motivated only by the desire to have the phone back.

Now let's talk about happiness. Of course, I want my kids to be happy. Who wants their kids to be miserable? Psychopaths. That's who. We semihealthy people love those children of ours more than anything, and one of our biggest goals is to raise them to be happy adults. But I've had to learn to pay attention to the difference between making them happy now, in this fleeting moment, and providing them with the tools to make themselves happy in the future. Immediate gratification suggests that life just showers you with whatever you want whenever you want it. But I worry that when my kids realize, *Oh, shoot! That's not the way it works,* they really will be unhappy, as in long-term miserable. The way I see it, I have to do my kids a favor by not always doing them a favor.

I'm going to be honest with you: I actually hope my kids don't go straight into their dream jobs, not because I don't want the best for them but because I *do* want the best for them. The best for them is learning that you can't and shouldn't go through life doing only what makes you 100 percent happy. Scrubbing toilets? Not my favorite thing. Paying bills? Hate it. Pap smears? Not fun in the moment, but probably a good idea in the long run. Obeying the speed limit? I'm not even addressing this. Pulling our weight, tackling our responsibilities—even when it's not a thrill ride—is what living in the real world involves, and I'd be a loser of a parent if I allowed them to avoid tasks they don't enjoy.

I want to teach my kids not to simply endure the mundane and boring and messy parts of life but to appreciate those moments. Happiness lacks depth without some discomfort to throw it into sharper relief, and if I don't allow my children to struggle, I won't give them the chance to feel the deep satisfaction of hard-won success. How many times have you seen the fancy toy your child begged Santa for collecting dust a few weeks after Christmas? But the bike they had to earn with months of vacuuming and yard work represents a lot of time and labor. Because its cost is more tangible, its value is, too. But it's not just about material rewards.

So much of the tedium of life is spent in service of others. Staying up all night with a sick child isn't fun for me; it's exhausting, often involves cleaning up a lot of disgusting bodily fluids, and doing an expert job of it won't make that dress I've been eyeing suddenly appear in my closet. But fetching cool washcloths for my kid's burning forehead makes someone I love feel a little less lousy, and that makes me feel good, too. What greater gift can I give my children than a work ethic that empowers them to find joy and meaning in even the most tiresome of tasks?

I try to make annoying things fun whenever possible. For example, my son Luka hates mornings more than anything (one of many traits we share), so for a while I would wake him up with his favorite music. There have been many mornings in our house that started with Nirvana dance parties. No matter how exhausted you are, the second you start headbanging to "Smells Like Teen Spirit," I can guarantee that you're fully awake. A little Kurt Cobain saved me a lot of hollering up the stairs to my sleepy preteen.

I love my kids, I enjoy my kids, and I have a lot of fun with my kids. But am I their BFF? Nope, nope, and nope. Frankly, I think there is something amiss about a forty-year-old and a seven-year-old being BFFs. In any other situation, that would just be creepy.

I've heard people insist that they can be their kid's BFF *and* their parent. But that's not how I define friendship. I don't tell my friends when to go to bed. I don't give my friends chores or consequences. And I don't wipe my friends' butts (but I suppose if it was some kind of unexpected, desperate emergency, I'd totally take one for the team). My friends don't need me in the same way my kids need me because my friends are already reasonable, responsible adults. I wouldn't open up to my kids about some of the stuff that I need to confide in my friends about—like divorce struggles or financial difficulties. My kids would be harmed by the unnecessary burden of that stress, and it would undermine the sense of security I believe they need to thrive.

Here's one way to look at it: if I ever walked into a new job or some other unfamiliar setting and there was no one in charge to guide me, set the expectations, or show me the ropes, I would be completely lost. But if someone I trusted who knew more than I did was in charge, I would feel safe. Same goes for the kids growing up in our homes, learning to function in the world. As much as they rebel and push back against rules, I believe they actually crave guidance and feel at ease knowing someone capable is at the helm.

I aim to be strict but fair. At the same time, when my kids screw up, I don't allow them to stew in their failures. I want to teach them that their failures are important and inescapable paving stones along the road to success. When my kids fail, I let them know I am proud of them for trying and prouder still when they dust themselves off and try again. And when my kids make mistakes that require reprimand, I make sure I tell them in word and deed that any consequences come from a place of love. Rules without love, communication, and genuine engagement will result in a relationship saddled with bitterness, distance, and rebellion. My kids need to know that they are really, really, really loved by me, *especially* when they are at their worst. Even when they are up on their soapbox, proclaiming that I am the meanest, most unfair mother in the whole world at 2:00 a.m. on a school night.

Sometimes, once things have cooled off, my kids can see the love behind my firm stance. For other conflicts, I may have to wait until they're thirty for that understanding to kick in. But it's okay. Because I'm in it for the long haul. The difference between being your kid's best friend and being their ally is the difference between being nice and being kind; the first is about a desire to be liked and the second is about a deeper desire to make a positive, lasting difference in someone else's life. My job is not to be liked by my kids. And I don't take it personally when my kids don't like me, because their well-being is more important to me than their opinion of me. My hope is that if I raise them well, with enough love and structure, then one day they'll grow up to be the kind of good and decent people I have the privilege of calling friends.

But before my kids become adults who can become my friends, they have to go through the teen years. Oh. My. Goodness. Need more reasons not to pursue being a BFF with your kid? How many healthy friendships have you been in with people who express zero interest in your existence, criticize your outfits, don't think of personal hygiene as a priority, and constantly tell you that your jokes are lame WHEN THEY'RE NOT or that your dance moves suck WHEN THEY DON'T FOR SURE?! Why would you want to be friends with someone who acts like you're an embarrassment and doesn't want to be seen with you in public so your entire relationship can take place only inside the walls of the home you're letting them crash in for free?

I was actually naïve enough to think that I would be really good at parenting teenagers. Right after college, I worked at a high school as a substitute teacher and the assistant theater director. I had a great relationship with those teenagers. They opened up to me about stuff. They came to me for advice. I remember foolishly thinking that the role I had in that high school was such great training for when I would have teenagers of my own. *I'm going to rock that part of motherhood,* I thought. But, you see, my relationship with those teens was easy because I WAS NOT THEIR MOM. Those kids were doing their best to show me their best selves and saving the full spectrum of their volatile emotional experience for the safety of their own homes. Atrocious behavior is like a twisted trophy that parents receive for doing a good job at letting their kids know they're loved unconditionally. Parenting is not for wusses.

I mean, seriously, parents, can we just raise a glass and down a shot of tequila to the fact that nurturing teenagers can be a nightmare? Forget baby showers! We should be thrown teenager showers! Because that type of shock to our system deserves a cake and gifts and then more cake. We probably didn't acknowledge it at the time, but when we fell for that oh-so-cute, sweet little baby, we were also signing up for the huge, overwhelming task of raising a teen. Nobody gets knocked up after thinking, *Wow, wouldn't it be adorable to have a hormonal, back-talking, eye-rolling, door-slamming teenager?* If I had known what it would be like, I would have registered for a therapist, not onesies, and I would've ended up with a very different baby shower.

Here are two things I've learned (and am still learning) that have helped me parent my teenagers with a little more compassion:

First, they actually do need me. Sometimes they are just too confused and moody and stressed-out and irritated and hormonal to realize it. When they are pushing me away, I need to stay steady. When they are trying to manipulate me, I need to be firm. And when they are acting completely unlovable, I need to love them even harder.

They also need me to shut up. They need me to listen more and talk less (which, trust me, is not easy for someone like me, who considers run-on sentences her daily workout). I've learned and failed and learned and failed and learned again that the best way to uncover what my teens need—the best way not to miss any red flags—is to stop talking *at* them, stop assuming I know what's going on, and instead pay attention.

You know your child. If your kid used to happily chow down on a big meal and suddenly they are sitting at the dinner table pushing their food around their plate, or if your restless night owl of a kid is suddenly sleeping all day, take note. We all break character once in a while. But a pattern of unusual behavior could be a symptom of something bigger going on with your kid that they might need help working through.

What if you want to change a dynamic with your kid that's been going on for years? When I've caught myself in bad patterns of behavior, I've tried to use those moments not only to atone for my mistakes and try to repair the relationship but also as opportunities to show my kids that people *can* change (which has the added bonus of bolstering my position when I'm asking them to make changes to their behavior). I'll sit down and say something like, "I've really screwed up. Throughout the years, I've overreacted when you've come to me with stuff because I was scared. And this is something I need to work on because my goal is to be there for you when you need me. I'll need you to be patient because I'm learning, but I'd like the opportunity to earn your trust back." Modeling accountability is a wonderful gift to give your child, and being honest and vulnerable may help them feel safer opening up to you.

If I don't want my teenagers to shut down, I have to listen closely to whatever language they're trying to communicate in until I've cracked the code. Because I can't help someone if I don't know the problem. I can't teach someone if I don't know what they need to learn. I can't guide someone if I don't even know they're lost. And the only way to know anything is to pay attention to the story they're actually telling and tune out the narrative I'm worried they might be drifting into or the character I want to cast them as.

When things get really confusing and I feel like I want to strangle one of my kids and we're escalating toward a full-on intense argument, I do my best to force myself to walk away. Because I believe the only thing harder than parenting a teenager is being a teenager. Refusing to engage in an unproductive back-and-forth and giving up on needing to have the last word doesn't mean I've lost power or even ceded the argument. Sometimes the most powerful tool a leader has is knowing when to walk away. I walk away because it's hard to think when I'm boiling with frustration and my defensive instincts have me coiled and ready to strike. I need to think, *Where is my teenager's behavior coming from? Is he saying this because he's scared? What does she actually need? What did I need at that age? What would have helped me?* There's always a story behind a child's actions. And if we can pay attention closely enough to figure out where the behavior is coming from, we will gain the insight to address the underlying pain or need instead of reflecting back the anger on the surface. When someone is angry, the root issue is that they are often actually scared. Instead of asking yourself, *What is she so mad about?* try asking, *What is she nervous about?* The answer to that second question gives you something you can work with. The minute you address their fears, the anger evaporates.

When I'm at my angriest, I aim to bite my tongue. And sometimes I slip up. Scratch that. I slip up all the time. I'll forget to walk away, or I'll raise my voice, or I'll name some crazy consequence that I can't even enforce and then quickly have to take it back, or I'll bring up something from the past that I swore I'd let go of. Then I'll have to stop and say, "I'm sorry. That's not fair. You're not the same person you were last year." I don't want to be judged now on the basis of everything I've ever done. And kids evolve much faster than we do. A year in the life of a teenager is like a decade of growth in the experience of an adult, so using the past as the metric by which I judge my kids doesn't do them any good. We get so mad at our teenagers for being irrational that sometimes we become irrational ourselves.

If you're facing down the dragon of parenting a teenager (and, honestly, let's throw toddlers into the mix, too), here's your mantra: *It's not personal. This too shall pass. I'm a badass. At least one brand of ice cream is on sale right now. I don't need my kids to be my biggest fans at all times.* Repeat that in your head all day while eating the ice cream. And then buy more ice cream.

Listen to me, lovely people. Please, for the love of everything that is good and holy and tastes like chocolate, do not feed me that whole "my kid is easy, my kid is perfect, my kid doesn't act like that" bit. Good for you. Throw yourself a freaking party. And also, how old is your kid? Five minutes? Is your kid even a human, or are we talking about your pet goldfish? Even if you did win the Powerball and wind up with a kid who's been a breeze, chances are that's got more to do with your kid than with your parenting, so you should thank your lucky stars and shut up about it already. Because most of us parents are challenged by our kids at times. And we're allowed to confidently admit that because, guess what. Challenging kids don't equal bad parenting. Or bad kids.

One morning as I was making breakfast, my then four-year-old, Ari, ran up to the kitchen counter and cheerfully told me he'd said a prayer for me the night before. My heart melted. "Really?" I asked. "Can you tell me what it was?" He nodded. "I prayed God would wrap you up with a big rope. And then he would tie the rope really tight. And then he'd put a lock on the rope and . . . and . . . throw the key away. Into the sea! And put you in JAIL. For a REALLY long time. Can I have some more milk, please?" Apparently, mean mommies who make their children go to bed when they don't want to, even when it's their bedtime, deserve to be punished. *Severely.*

But Ari wasn't the first to nonchalantly drop such a bomb in my lap. When my oldest, Luka, was around six or seven years old, he fired me. He told me I was fired. According to his standards, I wasn't doing my mom job correctly. And over the years, I've received feedback such as "I hate you!" from more than one child.

Let me remind you: it's not personal. Even incredible parents end up with kids who are asses. And even kids who are wonderful are asses some of the time. We need to be wise and creative and thoughtful with the things we can control, and in the decisions we make, the rules we set, and the way we love our children and react to them. But we also need to accept that we can't control everything or everyone all the time (nor should we), and our kids might make really bad choices—even heartbreaking ones—in spite of the time and effort we put into this parenting gig.

Too many parents fall into the trap of sorting themselves into boxes. "We're the strict family; we follow rules, and if someone falls out of line I'm going to call them on it," or "We're the fun family, and I want my kids to have a childhood filled with magic and delight!" But what children need most is to have a heady blend of structure and spontaneity. They need the rules and they need the fun, too. Sometimes they need to be held a little tighter and sometimes they need to be free to fall. When kids are little, there are times when you pick them up and save them because they are about to tumble down the stairs. Other times, you see the baby about to trip, and you have to let them go so that they learn how to stand up again when they tip over. Of course, the older they get, the trickier it becomes to identify which moments are for catching and which are for falling—and the stakes feel higher than ever.

As I've gone through the growing pains of parenting and as my parenting philosophy has emerged and evolved, I've learned to give my kids space to be themselves. In that same way, I've learned to lighten up. I've gotten more flexible with and more forgiving of myself. I started to celebrate the good intentions that drive my actions and to nurture and heal the pain and fear that often hide behind my missteps and mistakes. And all of that love and positivity I've given myself has transformed me.

Years ago, if I'd had to go through what I'm currently limping through with one of my kids, I would have spent every waking moment beating myself up, feeling like a loser parent. If I still had the mind-set I had years ago when I believed that I wasn't enough and that my children deserved better than me, this struggle would be so much harder and more complicated to shoulder.

But here is what I also know: I wasn't a completely different person back then—when I hated myself—from the person that I am now. It's just that my perception of myself was completely different. I focused on the negative. I didn't acknowledge my strength. I didn't give myself credit for how much I accomplished every day, even in the midst of my struggling.

What's helped me the most during these past few months is the certainty that I am doing the best I can. No, I'm not perfect. Yes, I've made mistakes. (Because . . . human!) But I am doing the best I can, and the stuff I don't know, I'm choosing to learn. I'm being honest. I'm being open. I'm getting help. I'm sitting down with a therapist. I'm taking me time. And, most importantly, I'm continually choosing to give myself more credit than criticism and more grace than judgment. This is so important that I wish I could grab every single one of you by the shoulders, look you in the eye, and say it to you over and over again until it starts to sink in: Please choose to give yourself more credit than criticism and more grace than judgment. You deserve it. And it will change you.

I'm done overlooking or undermining how much I actually do or how deeply I love. And I'm showing up. I don't want to run away or hide in denial or wrap myself in ignorance. As tough as life and parenting get, I want to show up for it. All of it.

So to that parent who has a kid with challenges that you could never have prepared for—keep showing up.

To the parent who is racing behind her kid at the playground, who has felt one step behind all day and like she just might lose it—keep showing up.

To the parent who is looking straight into his child's face and yet can't recognize him because mental illness has taken over his mind—keep showing up.

To the parent who is struggling with her own self-worth—keep showing up.

To the parent who is getting the eye rolls and the door slams and the "I hate yous"—keep showing up.

Keep showing up for your kid and, just as importantly, don't forget to show up and take care of the most important person in your child's life—you.

I am in the midst of some of the toughest struggles I've faced as a parent, and I'm guessing there will be more crying in public places, more challenges I've never rehearsed for, more struggles I could never have anticipated. But I know that I can break without being broken forever. And I know that finding my resilience, that doing what it takes to make a difference today, usually requires less effort than I'm dreading it will and brings less pain than I'm worried it will. Being what my kids need doesn't take the correct answer or the most brilliant idea or perfect parenting. Sometimes all I need to do is show up.

With all the other stories of struggle in this book, I know their endings. I can tell you those stories from start to finish, and I can see the lessons and the gifts those stories have given me. Because once a chapter ends, it's easier to see it as another meaningful, enlightening step that has contributed to my life's journey. But the truth is, I don't know how this particular chapter of my story will end. It's still in progress. So I'm going to just keep showing up. Eyes wide open, arms wide open, heart wide open. I'm here.

Acknowledgments

Writing a book, for me, has been a lot like labor and delivery without an epidural. Except no one handed me an adorable little baby at the end of it, which I'm not thrilled about. I've never considered myself a writer, and, as with anything else in life, I'm better with others—my life doulas—at my side in this process. I'd like to thank a few of these doulas who have been especially incredible birthing partners in bringing this book to life.

My husband, Philip, you had faith in my passion and my goals before I even fully did. Thank you for being so incredibly selfless and for all the sacrifices you've made so that I could take the time to pour my heart into these pages—all the dishes, laundry, and dog-poop scooping you've done after your own long, exhausting days of work, the days you've sent me off to write while you handled all things at home, and so much more. I can be pretty loud and obnoxious and you still find me adorable 97.2 percent of the time. I don't know how you have the patience that you have, but I'm eternally thankful for it.

My children, Luka, Matea, and Ari, I love you so much. You are the best parts of my life and my greatest teachers. Also . . . you're welcome. I didn't write ALL the stories I wanted to because I knew you'd be embarrassed about some of them, so I'm saving those for the next book. Kidding. Or not. Now go clean your room.

Mom, thank you for giving me life, but, more importantly, thank you for teaching me to give. Through watching you, I have learned the joy that comes from helping others. It is the best part of me and I owe it to your example. *Volim te neba visoko.*

Anna Sproul-Latimer, my literary agent, thank you for believing in this book when I had little faith that I'd ever be able to write it, for the pep talks and guidance, and for seeing me through this process. You've become so much more than an agent to me.

To my incredible editor, Laura Tisdel—from our first meeting, I felt like you were the right person to help me bring this book to life, and I was right. Thank you for challenging me, and for reassuring me when I started to doubt every thought and overthink every word. You're amazing and I'm so thankful this book brought you into my life.

Jo, you're one of the few people who know the stories in this book incredibly well because you walked through so many of them with me. It was such a gift to have you on call while writing, to help me think through some of my experiences and help me find the best way to put them on paper. For the past almost twenty years, you've been one of the first people I've shared my bad news with and one of the first I've shared the great news with. Thank you for being there for me from my worst days to my best, and loving me the same throughout it all. Your friendship is a gift I will never take for granted.

Cat, I still pinch myself that one of my favorite people and closest friends now also works with me. I adore you and can't wait to be roommates with you in a retirement home someday, making more penis-themed videos. Work never feels like work with you.

Judy, my sweet mother-in-law, I appreciate you for always so willingly stepping in to help with the kids, for all the delicious meals, and for never skimping on the butter when making those meals.

Julie Phifer, our amazing babysitter who now feels like family, thank you for keeping the kids alive and happy and the house from totally falling apart while I was bringing this book to life.

To my team at Creative Artists Agency, I love and appreciate you. Thank you for helping me grow and pushing me to take risks and recognize my own strengths.

Zach, I love you more than candy. Susan, thank you for the most creative "Writer's Survival Kit" package (and for birthing Zach). Amy P, thank you for welcoming me into your rock pad to write when I needed a change of scenery. Gillian, thank you for bringing fresh eyes to the words I put on the pages.

To all the rest of my family and friends, thank you for being an unbelievable support system. Your unconditional love and kindness mean the world to me.

To all my viewers and followers, many of whom remain complete strangers I have yet to meet, thank you for watching me and reading my posts and for letting me know that what I have to say resonates with you and means something in this sometimes fake and scary world. You are the reason I'm so passionate about what I do, and your support makes it possible. This book wouldn't exist without you.

There's so much good in my life, but the best parts of my life are the people in it. I'm thankful for each of you.

To chocolate and good crusty bread, thank you for being ever so reliable and never letting me down.